AFTER THE BELL

THE GERALD McCLELLAN STORY

By Wayne Lettice Lennon

warcrypress.co.uk
Wayne Lettice Lennon (c)

ISBN: 978-1-912543-02-1

'AFTER THE BELL 'THE GERALD McCLELLAN STORY' - Produced by wacrypress.co.uk (part of Roobix Ltd: 7491233) on behalf of Wayne Lettice Lennon Copyright © Wayne Lettice Lennon 2018.

Wayne Lettice Lennon has asserted his right as the author of this work in accordance with the Copyright, Designs and Patents Act 1988.

Original jacket illustration by James Ryan Foreman. Image inspired by various historical Kronk Gym images

Printed and bound in Great Britain by Clays, St. Ives

Find out more at: facebook.com/GeraldMcClellanstory/

NOTE: A donation from the sale of each publication will be made to the Gerald McClellan Trust

Today it costs approximately $70,000 per year to take care of Gerald and pay for the round-the-clock assistance that he requires. Astronomical medical bills and the costs of his yearly care have sadly exhausted all of the money that he has earned as a professional prize fighter. For this reason, Gerald and his family rely solely on donations to the Gerald McClellan Trust to care for him.

If you would like to make a tax deductible contribution to the Trust, please send check or money order made payable to Gerald McClellan Trust to:

Gerald McClellan Trust, C/O Fifth Third Bank, 839 E. Wyandotte, Freeport, IL 61032

You may also make a secure credit card donation to the trust via PayPal at: lisa@geraldmcclellan.com

For Casey xxx

'I have seen more fights than anyone in the world. I estimate I've seen somewhere around 60,000 fights live in my time…The best fight I ever saw was Benn/McClellan, without a doubt. We've not had another one [like it] since. The outcome was unfortunate with what happened to McClellan, but it was a tremendous fight.'

Mike Goodall, Ring Announcer, Ring Supplier, Boxing Expert and Commentator.

'Boxing is just show business with blood.'
Frank Bruno, Former Heavyweight Champion.

'I don't plan on being in the ring that long…I don't see anything other than a vicious knockout.'
Gerald McClellan, February 1995.

'He said to my dad, "I'm gonna hurt your boy." I don't mean to be disrespectful to him, but he was a very spiteful man. Things he did really were cruel. He had that kind of gangster image…I was not scared at all.'
Nigel Benn on Gerald McClellan, 2015.

'In the clearing stands a boxer and a fighter by his trade, and he carries the reminders of every glove that laid him down, or cut him 'til he cried out in his anger and his shame, I am leaving, I am leaving, but the fighter still remains.'
Simon and Garfunkel, The Boxer, Lyrics.

'It's entertainment, baby! That's all. Heroes and villains, angels and devils. Shit, if you didn't have Don King, you would have to invent him.'
Don King, Boxing Promoter.

About the author

Wayne Lettice Lennon was born in Dewsbury, West Yorkshire and raised in neighbouring Batley. He worked many jobs, including as a factory operative, window cleaner, waiter, call centre agent, leaflet distributor, salesman and marketing assistant before studying English Literature and Philosophy at the University of Leeds. He has previously written for the West Yorkshire Playhouse and Poetry and Audience Magazine. He lists boxing as one of the great loves of his life and proudly represented the same boxing club his father had fought for, twenty years earlier. His debut novel, *Life Before the War*, is still available through Warcry Press and many other major book suppliers.

Author's note

This is not a work of fiction. This book was put together from countless hours of my own obsessive research along with my own firsthand interviews wherever possible. Artistic licence has been taken in abridging certain conversations for the sake of cohesion and clarity, but nothing has been taken out of its perceived and intended context. This book remains a true account as reported, read and relayed to me. Any key secondary texts addressed or studied have been respectfully referenced in the back bibliography. No intentional infringement has been committed in any instance.

I would like to thank everyone who was kind enough to give me a personal interview for this publication. They include, but are not limited to, several former fighters, a Lord Mayor, a Neurosurgeon, a police officer, a journalist and many other relevant individuals on both sides of the Atlantic. Sincere thanks also go to the online platforms of *Boxing Legion*, *Boxing Exposure* and *Just Boxing* for their assistance in promoting this book. Keep punching, lads.

I would also like to offer very special thanks to Miss Lisa McClellan for her crucial input and for giving me many glimpses into her world. We may not have seen eye to eye every step of the way, but getting to know you has been an honour and a privilege. I respect you more than you will ever know. I am very grateful and wish nothing but the best for you and Gerald from the bottom of my heart.

Thank you again to my publisher Warcry Press and to my esteemed friend Sean Conway for supporting me when I really need it. Let's do this.

Wayne, December 2017

Contents

Introduction

'In war you have to be prepared to die. That's what boxing is.' Gerald McClellan, Thursday, February 23rd 1995. Two days before the Benn fight.

Darkness had fallen. In the two or three hours since the baying crowds had entered the venue, twilight had thickened into night. In the two or three hours since they had presented their tickets, left the bustling foyer bar and headed to their seats brimming with anticipation of the evening's entertainment, so much had changed.

They had come in droves. Men in tuxedos and dinner shirts, women in frocks and gowns; the glamorous and the gladiators separated by the width of a ring rope. The show now over, an army of fight fans exited the London Dockland's Arena. At once disturbed and exhilarated by the controlled carnage they had just witnessed, many would rush home to tell their loved ones how they had just been spectators at one of the all time great fights. Others, the London natives piqued with patriotism and adrenaline, the boxing aficionados who had booked hotels and travelled down especially for the occasion, would move on to the city's pubs and nightclubs in celebratory mood. They would sing the name of Nigel Benn long into the night.

Through the lamp-lit streets of the English capital, two separate ambulances sped on with sirens blurring. Time was of the essence. In the back of one, the victorious champion Nigel Benn had just regained consciousness. He had collapsed from pain and exhaustion on his way back to the dressing room, the paramedics quickly carrying him through a sea of delirious well-wishers. He had still been holding the precious championship belt across one shoulder as he passed out. His nose and jaw were fractured, his face swollen and bloodied from battle.

Sitting beside him now, his anxious girlfriend Caroline couldn't stop her tears. There had been other fights, of course, but none quite like this one. Nigel squeezed her trembling hand and smiled at her with bruised lips.

'You want to go out partying?' he whispered, half-joking. She managed a small laugh in spite of herself and let her tears flow.

In the other ambulance, Gerald McClellan had also regained consciousness. He looked around himself in fear and confusion. Still in his boxing trunks and boots, his hands bandaged, he was strapped to a stretcher. An oxygen mask was fastened to his face, a neck-brace preventing him from moving his head. A paramedic was busily suctioning a heart-monitor to his bare chest. Blinking rapidly, Gerald made out the figures of his corner-men, Stan Johnson and Donnie Pendleton, seated beside him. Hurt and bewildered, he managed to speak.

'What the fuck happen? I got knocked clean out, didn't I?

'You didn't get knocked out,' Stan answered him. He gave Gerald's hand a reassuring squeeze. 'You went down on one knee, you walked back to the corner, and you quit.'

Gerald refused to believe it. To be knocked unconscious was one thing, but he could make no sense of himself as a quitter. He looked at each of his men in turn: 'Motherfucker, you lying. Donnie, tell this motherfucker he lying!'

Gravely, reluctantly, Donnie shook his head: 'Sorry Gerry, but that's exactly how it happen.'

The ambulance sped on, bypassing the nuisance of red lights as journalists and photographers tailed them. By the time the ambulance drove into the emergency bay of the nearby Millwall hospital, a team of doctors, nurses and neurosurgeons was already waiting to rush him into emergency theatre. Hurt, but still conscious, Gerald quietly assured them he was alright, told them not to worry. He had no idea that his oxygen-starved brain was rapidly swelling against the inside of his skull, or that the pressure was irreparably destroying the crucial cells, circuits and nerve endings that made him who he was.

Minutes later, Gerald McClellan closed his eyes again. This time, he slipped into the ominous depths of a coma. This time, it would be many anguished days before he opened his eyes again.

A couple of hundred miles away in West Yorkshire, I had just watched the fight live on television. It had been gripping, pulsating, enthralling. I was twelve years old and had watched it with my dad. This was our thing. We watched all of the big fights, and some of the small ones. Boxing was a mutual obsession and a big part of our bond. My dad is a former fighter himself, and I would eventually lace up the gloves.

I grew up in a house where boxing magazines rested on the coffee table, legends like Hagler and Duran adorning the covers. Our cabinet in the living room was stocked with videos of all the great fights – Ali, Marciano, Ray Leonard, et al. We permanently had a heavy-duty punch-bag hanging from a ceiling hook on our landing. My brother Shaun and I would beat the crap out of it, when we weren't beating the crap out of each other. When fight nights like this came around, whether it was Tyson, Bruno, Naz, Eubank, Holyfield or 'Scrap Iron' Ryan topping the bill, my dad and I would load up with snacks, get comfy in front of the television and engross ourselves in the action. We knew the outcomes better than anybody.

I couldn't sleep that night. Of all the bouts I had seen up to that point, this one had been different. It is just part and parcel of life that most things never live up to their billing – books, films, TV shows, nights out, meals, even relationships – the higher the expectations, the bigger the eventual disappointment of the event itself. That often seems to be the case with boxing's big fights, too. This one was different. This one did not disappoint.

'Benn V McClellan' had been given all the hype and propaganda befitting a world title fight and then some. They had billed it as 'Sudden Impact' and for days showed images of the two warriors eyeball to eyeball on the television and in the newspapers. The anticipation was almost unbearable. And for once when the bell rang, the fight was even more thrilling than anyone could have hoped. It made the exaggerated, choreographed battles of the Rocky films look like mere tickling contests. As American commentator Steven Albert at ringside put it, 'This isn't a boxing match; it's a Hollywood script.'

The next morning as I was getting ready for school, my mind was still on the fight. Meanwhile, the fight and its aftermath were all over the television news. As it transpired, Gerald McClellan, the defeated American challenger, had been rushed to hospital in a critical condition. Whilst I had been tossing and turning in my bed, replaying the ring war over in my head, neurosurgeons had been operating frantically on McClellan's head in a desperate bid to save his life. I felt shocked, perhaps even guilty, at cheering Nigel Benn on as our British hero had somehow turned

4

certain defeat into incredible victory. I remember my dad saying, 'He'll be OK. He's tough.' I hoped he was right.

That fight never really left me. I had recorded the coverage on VHS tape and over the years I watched it more than any other in my ever growing collection. I felt emotionally involved somehow. As I grew older and the evolution of the internet put the world at my fingertips, I read and watched everything I could find about Gerald McClellan. Over time, I became as interested in his post-fight existence and in the efforts of his brave and brilliantly devoted sisters as I was in him as a boxer.

That night shook the sport to its core. But this is more than just a boxing story. It is a tragedy, a war story, a true-life fable of pain, despair, loss, struggle, betrayal, love, family, devotion and redemption all rolled into one.

Finally, as I began to forge the fledgling writing career I had always wanted, I knew theirs was a story I needed to tell. Nervously, tentatively, I contacted Gerald's sister, Lisa McClellan, over in the States. When she responded with her contact number, I was delighted. When she put me on the phone to the champ himself, I could hardly sit still. When she invited me out to the family home in Illinois, I wanted to cry with pride and call every member of my family. I could hardly wait to get writing, researching, exploring. Like a fighter tying his wraps, it was time for me to get to work.

I would like to dedicate this book to the McClellan family, to my family, and to anyone who has ever stepped inside a boxing ring.

1

Another Candle

'He ain't heavy; he's my brother.' The Hollies

Every year on Gerald's birthday, the McClellan family hold a dinner party. Every year, their closest friends, relatives and occasional special guests gather in a nice restaurant to break bread and celebrate the champ's life. They give thanks that he is still with them – another candle on his cake.

At home in the prelude, Lisa makes herself look pretty for the special evening. Once she has readied herself, she will run Gerald a bath. She will make sure the water's temperature is just right and she will help him into the tub. While he bathes himself, splashing and chattering incessantly, she will iron his clothes to flawlessness. When he is clean, she will help her big brother out of the tub and into a smart tuxedo. While she dresses him, Gerald will ask his sister where they are going.

Smiling, Lisa will bend towards her brother's ear and she will answer him, loud and upbeat: 'Tonight is your birthday party, Gerald. You remember?'

'My birthday party?' Gerald will ask her in surprise. 'How old am I?'

Lisa will answer him smiling: 'You're thirty, Gerald,' or 'You're forty, Gerald,' or 'You're fifty, Gerald,' or whatever the number is this particular year.

Together, Lisa and Gerald will wait outside for their ride to the party. In his tux and in his wheelchair, Gerald still looks sharp; he is still a handsome man. As the ride pulls up to collect them, his head will twitch around in search of his dear sister. He knows she will be somewhere close; she is always somewhere close. Sensing her presence beside him, he will look towards his sister through eyes that cannot see.

'Lisa, Lisa, Lisa,' he will say in agitation, 'where are we going?'

Lisa will bend and bow to her brother's eye-level, her smile never faltering, her tone as patient and pleasant as if she were saying it for the first time: 'Tonight is your birthday party, Gerald.'

'My birthday party?' Gerald will ask her, surprised. 'How old am I?'

'You're thirty, Gerald...You're forty, Gerald...You're fifty, Gerald...'

When they arrive at the venue, Lisa will wheel her brother into the function room. The congregation of well-wishers will applaud his entrance, the entrance of a champion. Startled by the sudden noise, the sudden energy, Gerald will jerk his head towards his sister. He knows she will be there; she is always there. Always.

'Lisa, where are we?'

Lisa will bend and bow towards her brother's ear. Her smile in place, her tone never betraying a shred of frustration or impatience, she will answer him: 'This is your birthday party, Gerald.'

'My birthday party?' Gerald will ask her, surprised. 'Lisa, do I look handsome?' His old male ego is still intact. He may not be able to see, but it matters still how he appears.

'You look very handsome,' Lisa will answer him, and she will be telling the truth.

Lisa will push the birthday boy to his place at the table. She will rest a plate of food in front of him, and with maternal care she will fasten a napkin beneath his chin. She will sit beside her brother and she will enjoy the company of their many guests. She will dine and she will converse and she will laugh.

In a few minutes, or perhaps in the next hour, or whenever the tarnished tape of his short-term memory suddenly runs out again, Gerald will turn towards his sister. He will look at his sister through eyes that cannot see and he will ask her where they are and what the occasion is.

Lisa will lean in towards her brother. Her smile will never falter; her voice will never shake: 'This is your birthday party, Gerald.'

'My birthday party? How old am I?'

'You're thirty, Gerald...You're forty, Gerald...You're fifty, Gerald...'

In the New Year of 1995, if someone had asked Gerald McClellan where he envisioned himself being by the time he turned fifty, his ambitious young mind must surely have danced with images of wealth and glory. He would no doubt be sitting figuratively in the Boxing Hall of Fame. On that point he would have been correct (Gerald was inducted into boxing's most honourable and elite class in 2007). Beyond that, he would almost certainly have seen himself as a multi-weight world champion. There would certainly be a hard earned multi-million dollar fortune stashed in the bank. His family and extended family would want for nothing. His three beloved sisters would probably be waited on hand and foot by servants at their beck and call. His parents, although separated, would be able to retire contentedly to their individual plots of comfort. When his children called to visit him with their respective mothers from their respective cities scattered across the Mid-West, they would surely be visiting him in a mansion of untold luxury – plaques and titles would adorn the walls along with framed snapshots of his greatest hits; all of the furniture would be green, his favourite colour, the colour of money. A fleet of flash cars would wait at his disposal in the sprawling garage. There would be a private gym, a swimming pool, a pen out back for his pride of pitbulls and possibly one out front for his harem of females. Gerald would probably be doing occasional guest slots as a television pundit for ESPN or HBO, maybe. If he foresaw any lasting injury marring his retirement years, he would probably have suspected a mean but manageable throbbing of his wrecking-ball hands – a legacy of knotted bones from blasting opponents unconscious. Life would be good. Living would be easy.

This is all a failed fantasy. This is not the life that Gerald McClellan lives now.

'Gerald has a good life,' Lisa states clearly, almost defiantly. 'It may not be the life he once had, but we make the most of what we do have.'

It sounds like Lisa really believes it when she says that. Perhaps she does. Perhaps she has convinced herself of it. There must be times though, in her most private, frustrated moments, where even she questions it. There must surely be quiet times when she stops between her endless chores and looks at Gerald as he sits in his armchair, the chair that might once have been a throne. Her big brother, two years her senior, the champ who was on his way to being pound-for-pound king of the ring in that most glorious pugilistic era of the 1990's; the good looking, super confident 'KO Kid' who would think nothing of spending upwards of $1000 on a casual shopping spree at the mall; the rising star who at age twenty-five paid for a $22,000 house in cash from his first decent contract; the brash and bold young warrior, who set off to London with sights set on destruction and came back blind; the beloved brother who can now never be left alone for more than a few minutes; the brain-damaged patient with ongoing annual medical bills in excess of $75,000 that completely dwarf the family's income and absorb any state benefits they are entitled to. By God, Lisa, there must be moments...

'God is always with us and He is always in control,' Lisa adds with continuing conviction. Lisa was studying at nursing school at the time her brother got hurt. She is a devout Christian, a church-goer, a believer. As a non-religious man myself, I ask her in all honesty how she can find gratitude towards the divine given the hand she was dealt. What God would plan this?

'I never even question it,' Lisa says. 'God is going to provide for me always.'

'You have a very strong mind,' I tell her, unsure of what else to say on the matter.

'No other choice,' she says.

No other choice.

2

Sudden Impact

*'Cry havoc, and let slip the dogs of war...' William
Shakespeare, Poet*

The prelude to all the big fights is The Tale of the Tape –
a detailed analysis of the two fighters facing off...

The show had been billed as 'Sudden Impact.' It was a
title which evoked images of speed and power; a rapid
collision, an abrupt climax, an explosive ending that could
come at any time and would probably come early.
Considering the records of the two fighters topping the bill,
the title was a very apt one.

Nigel Benn was the British hero and reigning WBC world
super-middleweight champion. He had turned professional
in 1986 and won all of his first twenty-two professional
bouts by knockout. Most of those contests had ended inside
the first two rounds with his opponents crumpled on the
canvas. By 1995, he had amassed thirty-five KO's from
forty-one victories. In the process, he had forged a proud
reputation as one of the best value for money fighters in the
business.

Equally impressive, the American challenger Gerald
McClellan had blasted his way to twenty-nine knockouts
from thirty-one wins. These included twenty devastating
knockouts inside the first three minutes alone. He had
made short work of journeymen and champions alike and
was being touted as *the* rising star of the fight game. As the
celebrated ring-doctor turned commentator Ferdie Pacheco
once said of McClellan, 'The guy fights like he's double-
parked outside the arena.'

So, the stage was set for a clash between two beasts
from opposite sides of the Atlantic. It was a battle which few
expected to last very long. A joint promotion between
flamboyant American matchmaker Don King and London

market-boy turned entrepreneur Frank Warren, it had all the hallmarks of a potential classic. Just analysing the two fighters' biographies in the build-up would send chills down the spine of any boxing aficionado.

Benn had grown up in Ilford, London, one of seven children of hard working British Barbadian parents. As with many or most pugilists, the story goes that he had been restless and troublesome as a youth. He grew up fighting and stealing his way through the unforgiving streets of East London. 'I never felt underprivileged, poor or resentful,' Nigel clarifies in his own autobiography. 'If I wanted something badly enough, I'd nick it…I never had any great moral dilemma for what I'd done…Most of the teachers at school were unanimous about my future; they reckoned I had none.'

Nigel eventually broke this cycle of petty crime by following one of his elder brothers into the British Armed Forces. Signing up in 1981, he would go on to serve over four years as an infantryman in the Royal Regiment of Fusiliers. This included a substantial period of service in Northern Ireland at the height of the country's ethno-nationalist conflict. The Army gave the young Nigel hard discipline and a sense of belonging. It also honed his natural ferocity.

'Platoon Sergeant Weaver was a bastard and a gentleman,' Nigel recalls of his early soldiering days. 'To see how tough we were, he'd order us to get down on our knees and stick out our chins. Then he'd walk by and crack jaws with his NCO's baton…If you could take it, you were tough and passed the test…I went into the Army a boy and came out a man.'

Benn had also come out of the Army as a boxer of serious potential. He was unbeaten at welterweight for two years in the First Battalion and had been outstanding enough to earn promotion to a post coaching other members of the unit's boxing team. Naturally, he had eagerly continued his amateur fighting career after leaving the forces and returning to civilian life. Back in London, he had joined the reputable West Ham Boys Club and trained under the expert guidance of Jimmy Tibbs and Dave Woodward.

In total, Benn lost only one of his forty-two amateur contests – a defeat which he later avenged. By 1986, he had captured the prestigious ABA title at middleweight – a national title held in the highest esteem by the boxing fraternity. From there on, Britain's biggest promoters were beating a path to Nigel Benn's door.

With his obvious marketability, Benn had risen rapidly through the professional ranks. Styling himself as 'The Dark Destroyer' and proclaiming himself to be 'Satan's right-hand man,' he had quickly captured the attention of the British public. He was everything a fighter should be: exciting, hard-hitting, dangerous, aggressive and he had fire in his eyes. All of this, along with his blue-collar, working class, no-nonsense persona, had helped him amass a fanatical home fan-base which would be bettered in subsequent years only by Manchester's 'cheeky chappy' hero, Ricky Hatton. Cashing in on his popularity, 'Big, Bad Benn' would even go on to have a rap song enter the British pop charts.

Benn was by no means a great technical boxer. He could appear flatfooted and he was often worryingly easy to hit. But what he lacked in scientific prowess, he more than made up for in other departments, not least courage and devastating power. As another member of his coaching staff, Kevin Sanderson, put it with a smile: 'He couldn't jab great, his feet were wrong. But heart and determination, you couldn't fault that.'

'I just love a good tear-up,' Benn liked to snarl. 'I fear no man.'

Nevertheless, Benn's meteoric rise had been interrupted. In his twenty-third professional bout his shortcomings had been cruelly exposed by technically brilliant British rival, Michael Watson. In one of the most eagerly anticipated domestic bouts of 1989, and one that delivered a frantic paced scrap from the first bell, the classy and composed Watson took Benn's Commonwealth title and his unbeaten record. He did it simply by standing his ground, punching judiciously and letting the overzealous Benn punch himself to exhaustion inside of six rounds. Dizzied by fatigue, Benn had been floored by a jab and could only watch groggily as the referee counted him out.

Cue a stream of ready criticism over Benn's perceived lack of stamina and his apparently low punch resistance. These were vulnerabilities which Benn's detractors would point out at leisure for the rest of his career. They were also a major factor in Benn's frequent placing as bookmakers' underdog, both at home and abroad. 'Underdog' was a label that Benn never worried about.

His invincible aura may have been badly dented by that first loss, but Benn's popularity with the public had not waned. Neither it seemed, had his desire to fight the best opposition available. The Dark Destroyer soon got back to winning ways, and in the spring of 1990, scored a massive victory in America to take the WBO World Middleweight title from 'Cobra' Doug Dewitt. Benn had bravely climbed off the canvas in Atlantic City and gone on to completely dominate the experienced New Yorker. He would return to Britain with a belt around his waist and a hero's welcome in wait.

Benn then added an emphatic first round knockout win over fearsome American Iran 'The Blade' Barkley. Barkley was a serious contender who had previously traded blows with all time greats such as Tommy Hearns and Roberto Duran. Interestingly, this victory over Barkley in Las Vegas had turned many stateside fight fans against Benn; the Brit appeared to land a glancing blow on Barkley after knocking the American down. In Benn's defence, the late, great voice of British boxing, Mr. Reg Gutteridge, commented: 'It's funny how the Americans don't like been on the receiving end of the rough stuff. They've been happy to dish it out for long enough.'

Continuing his winning streak, Benn also knocked out top contender Robbie Simms, the half-brother of legendary former champion 'Marvelous' Marvin Hagler. The presence of a tuxedo wearing Hagler at ringside made little difference to the outcome as Benn had it all his own way. By now, America's finest were surely beginning to detest any mention of the 'Dark Destroyer'. It would be back on English soil that Benn tasted defeat once again.

The most famous fights of Benn's career prior to 1995 had undoubtedly been his two meetings with his bitterest of rivals, the eccentric but exceptional Chris Eubank. The first of these epic battles, happening in 1990, still ranks as one of the biggest nights in British boxing history. Pitting brawler against boxer, the grudge match gripped the nation and saw Benn suffer a gutsy defeat. Again, Benn seemed to run out of gas and became an easy target for precision shots in the later rounds. The rivalry between Benn and Eubank continued to fester and they would meet again in 1993. This time, Benn managed a controversial draw, though most observers, including this humble writer, surely scored it in Benn's favour.

In between his two wars with his most hated antagonist, Benn had added another world title to his name. In 1992, the rejuvenated Benn had moved up to super-middleweight and promptly captured the more prestigious WBC version of the world title. He had wrested this crown by severely cutting open the eyebrow of crafty Roman fighter Mauro Galvano in front of a bitterly hostile crowd in Lazio, Italy. Galvano and his team had reduced the contest to a farce at its climax when, in desperation, they shamefully attempted to manipulate referee Joe Cortez into calling the fight off as a technical draw. Thankfully, with a little help from Barry Hearn at ringside, better sense prevailed and Benn was champion again.

Throughout all of this, Benn's personal life had also been far from settled. He had split from his first wife Sharron in 1993 and soon moved out to Los Angeles with his new partner, Carolyne. He would later admit to living a hedonistic, party lifestyle between training camps and to using copious amounts of alcohol and narcotics. In the wake of divorce, he had grown depressed at being separated from his children back in England. His mental state was such that he had even sought the aid of celebrity hypnotist Paul McKenna to help him focus and overcome bouts of anxiety.

Benn had finished 1994 by winning a lacklustre twelve round bore against Paraguayan mandatory, Juan Gimenez. That fight never really caught fire – at least not inside the ropes. The restless Birmingham crowd did briefly break into an ugly disturbance in a bid to entertain themselves. Chairs and punches were thrown before police intervened. Nevertheless, Benn retained his title, even with one of the judges scoring it as a draw.

So, by the turn of 1995, Nigel Benn was thirty-one years old. He still held his precious WBC title and he was still the consensus fans' favourite of Great Britain. However, it was also a widely shared opinion in boxing circles that he was past his prime, past his best and that all of those gruelling battles had taken much out of him. Critics believed that his often highlighted stylistic vulnerabilities would soon conspire to end his reign. Now more than ever, it seemed like a good time to catch Benn. Now more than ever, it seemed like a good time for a hungry and self-assured young challenger to meet the aging warrior-king.

Challengers did not come much hungrier or more self-assured than Gerald McClellan. They did not come much more dangerous either. As once described by the great Reg Gutteridge, McClellan was simply, 'A freak of nature.' His own corner-man, Stan Johnson, would later label McClellan 'The most violent man ever to put on a pair of gloves.' This was the kind of hype preceding the handsome young American as he boarded a plane bound for England.

Originally hailing from Freeport, Illinois, in America's Mid-West, the self-styled 'G-Man' was a product of Detroit's famed Kronk Gym. He was a pupil of the now late, great Hall of Fame trainer of champions, Emanuel Steward. He was a stable-mate of multi-weight world title winner Tommy 'Hit Man' Hearns, as well as world heavyweight titlist Michael Moorer and top ranked contenders such as Oba Carr and Tarick Salmaci (the latter of whom was kind enough to grant me a personal interview for this publication).

As an amateur, McClellan had beaten the outstanding Roy Jones Jr. in a bout at the prestigious Golden Gloves tournament. Jones would go on to win multiple professional world titles in four different weight classes and is regarded by many as the greatest pound-for-pound fighter of all time. Still, even Jones, speaking some years after his amateur defeat to McClellan, insisted he had no desire to face the G-Man again in the paid ranks. One could hardly blame him.

Even the explosive heavyweight legend 'Iron' Mike Tyson, a name scrawled high on any respectable list of big punchers, had been quick to single-out McClellan as a fledgling star. During an interview from his prison cell whist incarcerated for sexual assault in the early '90's, Tyson was asked by Larry King which contemporary fighters he presently rated. Without hesitation, Mike had quietly noted, 'There's a new gentleman from Detroit – McClellan or McClean, I think his name is…I've seen some highlights of him and he looks like a dynamo.'

That was a fair assessment, and it seems fitting that before long many were describing McClellan as a 'mini Mike Tyson.' The comparison made perfect sense; the rapid-fire hand speed, the power to crumble a man with one shot, the fluidity of lateral upper-body movement designed to draw maximum force into each punch. And, of course, there was the apparent natural penchant for violence. Like Tyson, McClellan seemed to enjoy inflicting punishment on his opponents. Like Tyson, McClellan was made to fight.

By age twenty-five, McClellan had captured two world titles and was striking fear into the hearts of all sane contenders operating anywhere around the 160lb mark. In 1991, he knocked out Ugandan Olympic medallist John 'The Beast' Mugabi with consummate ease, winning in the first round to claim the vacant WBO world middleweight title. Then, in 1993, he scored a brutal fifth round knockout over the ferocious and much feared champion, Julian 'The Hawk' Jackson, to take the WBC middleweight crown. That brief but thrilling battle saw McClellan land a neck-snapping left-hook to send the top half of Jackson's body hanging horizontal outside the ring ropes. It was the kind of shot that would have knocked an elephant off its feet. McClellan would later prove that victory was no fluke when he annihilated Jackson again, this time in just seventy-eight scintillating seconds of their rematch; that was seventy-eight seconds *including* the ten-count. By the end of 1994, Gerald had racked up twenty first round knockout victories – 'a dynamo,' indeed.

So, by the turn of 1995, it seemed that the world and all its spoils rested in Gerald's gloved hands. Having struggled to make the 154lb limit at middleweight for his last few fights, McClellan decided he would put on six pounds and move up. With his phenomenal power and natural aggression, he saw nobody in the 160lb super-middleweight division to worry him at all. If he could beat Benn, as most predicted he would, he would become a two-weight world champion. If he could beat him in typically ferocious style, then surely the future knew no limits.

It was supposed to be so easy.

3

An Englishman, Irishman, Frenchman and a Yank

'There was violence in the air all around the fight.' Brendan Ingle, MBE, Boxing Coach

He couldn't just fight. Gerald McClellan looked the part, too. Caramel skinned with smooth, even features, a pencil moustache riding his top lip, he could easily have passed for a young Apollo Creed. Gerald was twenty-seven years old and fast approaching a potent physical prime. Tall for a middle-weight at just over six feet, his lean but muscular frame was decorated by the odd tattoo, including one bearing the name and caricature of his beloved pet pitbull, Deuce.

Gerald arrived in the UK carried on a wave of hype and media attention – the American monster invading British shores. Dressed in a sharp, mustard-coloured suit and gold chain, he strolled into London's Peacock Gym nodding polite greetings at the gaggle of press photographers who had gathered outside to catch a glimpse. There, he would be finalizing his preparations for fight night. No one could possibly imagine that it would be his last.

Gerald's manager, the most powerful man in boxing history, Don King, was never far behind. He smiled that slimy smile and waved tiny American flags at the cameras while repeatedly touted his man as a miniature Mike Tyson. Gerald's small entourage of young, confident black males accompanied him everywhere, each exuding a practiced, menacing bravado. This team intentionally added to the contest's sharpening edge of Anglo-American rivalry by wearing white t-shirts emblazoned with the Stars and Stripes. In their thick Illinois accents, they would call out boasts and warnings aimed at Nigel Benn, as their own fighter skipped rope or drilled the pads with expert ease.

Supposedly at the helm of these proceedings was the outlandish head coach, Stan Johnson. Barrel-chested with hair straightened to his shoulders, Johnson strutted around the gym wearing body-armour and his trademark cap (not a casual baseball cap or fashionable stocking-cap, but the type of hat an aeroplane pilot or sea-captain would wear. There will be more on him later).

While the shirtless Gerald flexed his muscles narcissistically in front of the floor-to-ceiling mirrors, or pounded the heavy-bag with hard shots, a tirade of loud, truculent rap music thumped from a nearby stereo; angry strains of Ice Cube and Tupac providing the soundtrack to each session. Whenever Gerald broke off from punching and posing to speak to the present English journalists, he fixed his steely eyes on the interviewer. He answered their questions politely, but with a measured devilment in his tone. He was composed, in control.

When told by one interviewer that many now regarded him as the second best pound-for-pound fighter on the planet, intending it as a compliment, Gerald licked his lips, struggled not to smile and said, 'Who do they say is number one?'

When the same reporter brought up Gerald's love for a certain breed of dog (he had recently posed for press shots in a hotel lobby with two of his pets straining at the leash) Gerald replied matter-of-factly, 'Pitbulls are the only dog that remind me of myself; just real aggressive; don't take nothing off nobody.'

Brash, bold, moody, posturing and completely confident, the whole demeanour of the McClellan camp only fuelled the unbearable anticipation. By show time, the excitement had reached fever-pitch. It would take some living up to.

It is unlikely that McClellan had ever come across an atmosphere like it. It is certain he had never fought in an atmosphere like it. The noise around his two explosive battles with Julian Jackson had been mute by comparison. Over twelve-thousand screaming Englishman, a scattering of celebrities, several renowned boxers enjoying being on the outside of the ropes for once, Barry McGuigan in a tux, Frank Bruno in a bright orange suite, Prince Naseem Hamed, Gary Newbon, Jimmy Lennon Junior, John McRirick, Don King, half the cast of Eastenders, several professional footballers and all of the most esteemed sports commentators from across the globe had gathered with drenched appetites. It was the kind of din usually reserved for a football derby day. Fittingly, the majority of Millwall F.C.'s hooligan firm and several known London gangsters and villains had also reportedly added to the numbers.

'There was violence in the air all around the fight,' Brendan Ingle would tell an interviewer years later. Wiley old Irishman Ingle, veteran trainer of world champions such as Nazeem Hamed and Johnny Nelson, had been given the duty of operating as McClellan's bucket-man that night. 'It was like Rumble in the Jungle,' he said.

Danny Flexen, the former publishing manager for *Boxing News*, was also in the crowd that night. He later wrote: 'The atmosphere was rabid and violent, as if association with such a brutal fight had transcended the fight and permeated the crowd.'

Like a true champion, McClellan was unfazed by the blood-thirsty intensity of the gathering, unperturbed by their passionate support for his opponent. He limbered up in the dressing-room, rap music blasting from a stereo, watching his own image in the mirror as he threw hooks and crosses at the air. Stan and Donnie stood by and watched their man, their boss. They were mere props in this, the Gerald McClellan Show. The champ had even fastened his own hand wraps because he didn't have faith in Stan and Donnie's ability to do it properly, the way Emanuel Steward used to. It didn't matter. In less than an hour he would be back at the hotel sipping champagne, a new belt resting on the dresser and a nice female resting beside him.

Testifying to Gerald's pre-fight focus, coach Stan Johnson recounted later how on leaving the dressing room he had asked Gerald if he wanted to carry out the commonplace athletic ritual of saying a prayer. According to Johnson, Gerald had replied dismissively, 'You wanna get fucking religious?' Johnson took that answer as a no, and with that they set off for the ring.

Maybe God was watching.

With Don King marching a few steps ahead of him, flags still waving, Gerald strolled down the aisle, a warrior immune to nerves or fear. A green and gold gown matched his trunks (he had refrained from wearing his familiar Kronk colours of gold and red - he and Kronk mentor Emanuel Steward had recently parted company on unpleasant terms).

Gerald tilted his chin and pursed his lips. He kissed the blood-red glove of his right hand and dog-eyed the television cameras; a showman oozing confidence and menace in equal measure. He paused and spit on the ground before bobbing between the ropes. He kissed his right hand again – the hand he called his 'Money Maker' –

and raised it towards the crowd. They responded with a confrontational roar – welcome to England. Throughout it all, the deafening boos and hisses made his entrance music inaudible. It was enough to break goose-bumps on a dead man's flesh.

Gerald bounced on the balls of his feet. He threw a few steady practice shots at the London air to loosen up. His team waved their nation's flag and taunted the crowd with raised arms. Stan Johnson stood with arms folded, an image of complacency. And then it was time for Nigel Benn.

The trademark chimes of iconic London bell-tower 'Big Ben' preceded the home fighter's appearance at the head of the aisle. Their deep toll provoked a chorused roar sufficient to shake the Isle of Dogs. Spotlights darted across the packed arena, neon flashed crazily from all angles, pulses quickened.

Flanked by Union Jack flags, Benn stepped from a cloud of illuminated effect-smoke. Dressed in sinister black trunks with a matching cowboy-style poncho, his hair a forest of short, twisted dreadlocks, he came out waving his right hand and bopping his head to the music. Corner-man Dennie Mancini paraded the green and gold WBC championship belt aloft, as if to say 'Come and get it.' Peter DeFreitas and Kevin Sanderson jostled for space at either side of their fighter, the latter chomping furiously on chewing-gum. 'It was scary,' he would admit years later, 'I'd never known anything like it.'

'The roof just came off,' Benn remembered, 'I felt like Spartacus going to the arena to fight to the death.'

Benn skipped through the ropes, head still bopping and fist pumping the air like he'd just stepped onto a nightclub dance-floor. The chanting, singing and shouting never relented for a second. As the preliminaries were played out, the national anthems observed, Benn shook off his poncho and eyeballed his challenger. 'His arms didn't look bad. His legs looked skinny,' he said later. 'I wasn't scared.'

Benn's own physique had clearly been hammered into peek condition. Globing shoulders bolted his neck to his body. His stomach muscles resembled stacked breezeblocks. The veins of his biceps throbbed with adrenaline. Pacing the ring like a caged lion, he looked ready. He always looked ready.

As tradition dictates, the two fighters were brought together centre ring to receive the final instructions. This is common practice in boxing throughout the amateur and pro ranks across the world. It gives the two fighters and their respective chief seconds chance to ask any last ditch questions they might have – no one ever asks any. It is also a point at which a fight at any level can be won or lost before a punch is thrown. Nose to nose, eyeball to eyeball with the man who is about to have legal license to attack you, any mere mortal can suddenly realise there are other places he would rather be. Mike Tyson, in particular, was exceptional at breaking a man's spirit with his dead-eyed glare before the opening bell. That was never going to happen here. Benn and McClellan both thrived on such moments of controlled terror (great boxers are truly exceptional humans). Neither man so much as blinked.

The pre-fight nose-to-nose is also a final opportunity for the referee to stamp his authority on proceedings. Of course, the boxers already know the rulebook long before 'the third man' summons them to hear it relayed. Whether they choose to abide by those rules is another matter, and that is where the referee earns his place. The chief official is not an ornamental piece or a mere spectator at close quarters. He is absolutely integral to the action. He needs to be assertive, authoritative, concise and absolutely crystal clear in every command he delivers inside the ropes. Communication is vital. He is, after all, the final adjudicator over two muscular men, both skilled in violence, who are about to professionally assault each other. Few positions in any walk of life hold more responsibility. His performance can be the difference between life and death. It is that simple.

The referee calling Benn and McClellan to the battleground's centre was a Frenchman. Parisian Alfred Asaro was short with a bouffant hair-do. Prior to that February night, he had officiated over only one previous world title fight – a flyweight contest which had been staged in Japan. Perhaps more significantly, he could not speak English at even a basic level.

As he delivered his final instructions to the fighters, Asaro made hand gestures and tapped his own forehead to fill in the many gaps left by English words missing from his vocabulary. Were it not for the tragic outcome of what was about to ensue, then even the keenest of repeat analysts of this fight might never have noticed this lack of communication skill. We would have had no cause to. But, as events unfolded, Mr. Asaro was about to turn in one of the most bizarre refereeing performances ever recorded.

Some years later, McClellan's corner-man Stan Johnson would state, 'We got a fight in England, where both fighters speak English. Can't we get a fucking referee who speaks English?'

In response to this, Asaro had given his own interview. Speaking in French, naturally, he stated, 'There is no duty to speak English in order to referee a fight. I can give

25

instructions – high, low, break, fight – like this.' Again, he used his trusty hand signals to illustrate each point.

Boxing writer, Gerald's friend and occasional fundraiser, Jake Donovan, gave as precise and accurate an assessment of Asaro's performance as one is likely to find when he said, 'To be a referee, it is required that you do some officiating, to keep the action clean and to offer an unbiased and policed presence. Asaro did none of this. Instead, he constantly pushed Gerald back whenever breaking up the two fighters. He stood in between the two fighters for far too long on every break. He stepped in and broke apart the fighters seemingly every time that Gerald would move in for the kill. He warned McClellan for infractions that weren't even committed, or at least not by him.'

In the immediate aftermath of the Benn Vs McClellan fight, the under-fire Asaro would obsessively cut out and keep every news article relating to the contest. He would also come to cherish a letter of support from the French Boxing Association. Roughly translated, the presiding message of that letter read, 'There is no blame on you. Be brave.'

Alfred Asaro would continue working as a professional referee for many years beyond that February night. In 2011, he received an award for services to boxing from the FBA.

To date, Mr Asaro has never contacted the McClellan family. My attempts to contact both himself and the French boxing authorities for comment on this publication received no response.

4

Round By Round

'Once the bell goes, it's you and the other guy. None of your supporters can help you.' Nigel Benn.

Round One:

Sudden impact, indeed - Benn stood his ground for all of thirty-six seconds. McClellan came out firing with bad intentions. A right hand to the ribs got Benn's attention and McClellan backed him up to the ropes. The challenger threw spear-like shots with both hands, every single one a power punch. Few landed cleanly, but McClellan hit hard enough that even the grazing shots rattled the champion. Benn ducked low beneath the waistline, frantically rolling the top half of his body from side to side, desperately trying to avoid the onslaught. McClellan stayed on top of him, firing punches downwards. Benn must have felt the wind off the shots that barely missed him. A barrage of heavy head shots saw Benn sink almost in slow motion through the middle of the ropes. Another right hand smashed into the joint between his jaw and his throat (Benn would later describe feeling the ligaments of his neck stretch and confirmed that no other fighter he'd ever faced could match this man's punching power).

Benn lay outside the ring ropes like a turtle flipped onto its shell. He had almost landed on the desk of the British television broadcasters at ringside. ITV favourite Gary Newbon patted him on the back as though urging him to get up. Benn didn't know where he was. Flash-bulbs sparked around the arena. The crowd stood as one. It looked to be over already. Perhaps it should have been.

'We thought this might happen,' British commentator Reg Gutteridge groaned pessimistically.

But Benn got up. He was groggy and embarrassed, dazed and clumsy, but brave as ever the old lion stepped back through the ropes. Already, with the fight less than a minute old, a moment of cataclysmic significance was unfolding. This would be a pivotal moment in the fight and in Gerald's life – a decision that the destiny of many would hinge on. The referee's count had reached only eight. Some might call that a slow count. Certainly, Stan Johnson in McClellan's corner was perplexed that the fight wasn't stopped there and then. He screamed from the corner, 'Know the fucking rules! What the fuck kind of refereeing is that?' Meanwhile in the neutral corner, the raging McClellan punched the air in frustration. He too believed he had made it another quick night's work.

So, was it a slow count? Should this fight have been over there and then? With the great benefit of being able to rewind and replay that knockdown at leisure many, many times, it is this writer's humble assessment that Benn was back on his feet by the count of nine, but not back in the ring until the count of eleven. Granted, the referee was performing in the most heated of moments, with twelve-thousand people screaming in his direction. But such pressure is part of his job. He was there to take charge.

WBC rules in the event of such a knock down are slightly ambiguous. The rulebook states: 'If a fighter falls outside the ring and ring apron, he will have 20 seconds to come back to the ring without assistance, unless the referee orders it.' – Taking this into account, Benn was clearly outside of the ring ropes. He did not, however, fall clear of the ring apron completely. Even if he had been set to plummet clear of the ring in its entirety, the press desk positioned just a few inches below canvas level would have prevented him from reaching the concrete. Conclusively, Benn was not entitled to a twenty second count. If he was not back on his feet and ready to fight by the count of 'Ten', then the contest should have been over.

Somehow though, the Frenchman had only counted to 'Huit' by the time Benn clambered back into the arena. When all is said and done, it is only the referee's count that matters. Regardless of his count's accuracy, if Asaro had not reached 'Ten' by the time Benn was ready to resume action, then he had no reason to stop the contest at that point. Even if the official Time Keeper at ringside, the same individual who rings the bell to end and commence rounds, had reached 'Ten', it would have taken a brave individual to try and intervene in these circumstances. Benn gets the benefit of the doubt.

'We were lucky,' Benn's corner-man Kevin Sanderson admits with a shrug. 'Sometimes, you need a bit of luck.'

Benefit of the doubt may vindicate the referee up to that point, but I can find no explanation in any rulebook to warrant his following actions. Asaro wiped off Benn's gloves against his shirt and seemed happy to let the fight continue. But then, rather than stepping out of harm's way to let battle commence, Asaro strangely positioned himself between the two fighters and pushed McClellan back repeatedly as the American tried to proceed. This allowed the dazed Nigel Benn four or five extra seconds of invaluable recovery time.

When Asaro finally did let McClellan get back to work, it wasn't for long. As Benn clung on for dear life around

McClellan's neck, Asaro parted the two fighters and again pushed McClellan back with both hands against his chest. McClellan himself could be seen chastising the referee in bemusement as he attempted to push passed him.

What I personally find most interesting about this brilliant and bizarre opening round is the difference in perspectives between the British and American television coverage. Whilst British ITV commentators Reg Gutteridge and Jim Watt only briefly noted Asaro's overbearing presence, their American counterparts were rightly incensed by it. Englishman Gutteridge quietly stated, 'The French referee is pushing McClellan off,' and his Scottish colleague Watt added, 'The referee has been very kind to Benn. He gave him a conveniently long count and he's trying to hold him off, but this man will not be denied.' Meanwhile Ferdie Pacheco, covering the bout for Showtime Sports in the States, was yelling in exasperation: 'What is this guy doing? Does he think he's refereeing an amateur fight?'

Asaro's inexplicable actions continued throughout the round. Again, as McClellan pushed relentlessly on looking for the finish, the referee stepped between him and his target without reason. He made incoherent sign language towards Benn, provoking Jim Watt to deduce, 'It's as though he's trying to help him survive this round.'

And survive Benn did, by the skin of his teeth. As the bell sounded, the British fighter staggered back to his corner. The justly infuriated McClellan pointed and shouted dissent at the referee. A fourth consecutive first round knockout win had been snatched from him.

Round Two:

As Nigel Benn staggered back to his corner disorientated, he must have felt like he had already done twelve rounds. But in a stroke of managerial genius, his corner-man, Dennie Mancini, used reverse psychology to boost his man's morale.

'Bloody Hell, Nige, you've got him in trouble here, mate!' Mancini lied. It was exactly what Benn needed to hear. It lifted his spirits through the haze and puffed out his chest. It was a white-lie that made all the difference. Benn got up off his stool and came out swinging.

Still, the referee Asaro felt the need to intervene. He stepped between the fighters, tapping his own forehead and making weird hand gestures, prompting Gutteridge to remark, 'He's a bit of a fussy referee, this European.'

With his head beginning to clear, Benn began to push forwards. It was untidy and scrappy, but McClellan began to be a bit more judicious with his punches. The American danced smoothly on his toes and fired out a piston-like jab, looking to create openings for the big right hand. Benn fired back though, landing a couple of good left hooks that drew roars of approval from the crowd. On the front row at ringside, Frank Warren, Prince Naz Hamed, Benn's father Dixon and the towering Frank Bruno led the cheers.

'I was so focused on the fight,' Bruno would say later, 'that Mickey Mouse and Batman could have been sitting beside me and I wouldn't have noticed.'

Suddenly, McClellan was the one grabbing and holding. No longer having things all his own way, he also complained to the referee about a rabbit punch to the back of his head. Asaro took the cue and gave Benn another set of rebuking hand gestures.

By the end of the round, Benn had taken the centre of the ring and landed more left hooks with skill and composure. McClellan skipped a retreat on the back foot, but still looked dangerous as he launched wild rights. As the bell sounded, Benn pumped his fist towards the crowd, as if to say 'I've got this.'

Round Three:

A short right uppercut inside the opening seconds of the round seemed to startle McClellan. A left hook rocked him back on his heels. The American couldn't help but show respect for Benn's tenacity by visibly changing tactics; he was no longer unloading bombs indiscriminately, but boxing on his toes behind a measured jab. A solid right hand breeched Benn's defence and caught him on the chin, but he took it and marched forwards.

As the two fighters came into a clinch, McClellan's mouthpiece began to protrude. For the remainder of the round, it would slide forwards until it was almost hanging out. Nevertheless, he caught Benn with a long right cross and finished the round the strongest of the two.

Round 4:

The round started with Benn stalking and McClellan and firing off shots from the outside. Still, that mouthpiece seemed peculiarly advanced in the challenger's mouth. Benn began lunging into his shots and found some success with both hands. The crowd roared him on. Frank Bruno banged on the ring apron and bellowed encouragement. Reg Gutteridge now described the tiring McClellan as 'A sailor in a storm hanging on to the mast.'

It was a scrappy round and the referee gave Benn another warning relating to the back of the head, but Benn landed the cleaner shots throughout.

Round 5:

McClellan came out looking revitalised and went head hunting with power shots. Still, that mouthpiece hung oddly beyond his lips. Stubbornly, Benn stood in front of the American and returned fire with fire. Reg Gutteridge commented now, 'I think McClellan is a bit shocked, but Benn has the heart of a lion...That gum-shield is hanging out, almost like he's spitting it out.'

McClellan looked composed on the back foot, picking his shots carefully, but still that mouthpiece looked to be on the verge of falling out completely. Was Gerald struggling to suck in enough oxygen? Was his nose damaged? Was it caused by a sudden onset of nerves at the ensuing tougher-than-anticipated battle? We can only wonder and never know. Either way, the pace of the fight showed no signs of slowing. As the bell sounded to end the round, the body language of both men suggested that they were beginning to feel it.

Round 6:

In the interval, British television coverage cut to a ringside interview with Prince Nazeem Hamed. Naz was quick to praise his fellow Brit: 'Nigel has taken the punches and now he's coming back with war,' said the then featherweight champion, '[McClellan] has blown himself out...believe me, it's Nigel's night now.'

Early in the round, Asaro gave Benn another telling off, this time for holding and hitting. McClellan began chopping away with hard shots to head and body. Incredibly, Benn took them and actually waved at the crowd, as if to gee them up even further. At ringside, Frank Bruno continued to roar support for Benn.

Benn pinned McClellan in a corner and peppered him with close range shots. McClellan spun away to take the action back to the centre of the ring. A long range right hand to the jaw from Benn finally sent McClellan's loose mouthpiece flying out of the ring. The imminent sounding of the bell saw Benn whack McClellan with three intentional right hands and then glare at his opponent with contempt. It had become a street fight. McClellan took the punches and responded only with a confused glance, as the referee stepped in. Asaro raced across the ring to reprimand Benn for the illegal punches on the bell. Benn bowed by way of apology and returned to his corner.

As he trudged back to his own corner, McClellan for the first time began to look dejected. His fire seemed to be extinguishing.

Round Seven:

The disparity between the two corners during this interval spoke volumes. In Benn's corner, the champion looked alert, his team practically bouncing with adrenaline as they massaged their man's muscles and rattled off instructions at him. Across the ring, a close up camera shot of

McClellan showed an unfamiliar look of reluctance on his face. Stan Johnson was talking to his man and simultaneously working his eyebrow with an endswell to prevent bruising. McClellan glanced across the ring and spit on the canvas as he waited for the bell to resume action.

A straight right hand stunned Benn and as he leaned forwards, McClellan struck him intentionally at the back of the head. Benn didn't complain and the referee let this go, but then seconds later the official found need to intervene again. This time, he separated the fighters and told them both off for reasons known only to himself.

Benn began to show signs of fatigue here, and McClellan began to tee-off with heavy shots hoping to finish it. It was a real see-saw battle. Still, that mouthpiece hung from his mouth. McClellan dominated with the cleaner work, but Benn finished the round with a flurry that shook the American.

Round Eight:

On his stool in the interval, McClellan appeared tired. He breathed heavily and gulped water that Stan Johnson squirted into his mouth. But Benn, too, was beginning to show signs of weariness.

McClellan began backing Benn up, his mouthpiece still protruding. At ringside, Gerald's promoter Don King was now on his feet, watching with avid interest. It wasn't quite going to plan, was it? It had never been meant to last this long.

McClellan landed a right to the body and then a long range right to the head that sent Benn staggering backwards into the ropes. McClellan followed him like a predator and threw everything but the kitchen-sink in search of the finisher.

Somehow, Benn swung back and landed two hard shots. Somehow, McClellan responded with more fire of his own. The crowd could hardly contain itself. There had never been a fight like this. This was something else.

Benn stumbled back into a corner; McClellan pursued him with a marauding attack. Benn swung a wild left that missed by a mile. His own body weight took him to the canvas, exhausted. The referee scored it as a knockdown, but Benn was bravely up at the count of four.

McClellan moved in again, surely sensing that he might finish it. But again, Benn somehow mustered up the strength to fight back. At the sounding of the bell, the crowd was delirious with primitive delight. This was something special, something primeval, something beautifully vicious.

'We promoted this one as "Explosive",' Gutteridge remarked, 'but I tell you what, we didn't promote it enough!'

Round Nine:

This was unchartered territory for McClellan, having never had a fight previously go beyond eight rounds. As though to lift his fighter's morale, corner-man Stan Johnson assured McClellan that he was winning: 'He cannot win this fight!' he yelled. The truth was that most score cards now had it balanced on a knife-edge. McClellan was in front, but it could still go either way.

McClellan landed a couple of right hands. Asaro stepped in briefly with more unnecessary interruptions in his mother-tongue. Benn kept pushing forwards valiantly, even as McClellan speared him with measured straight rights.

Again, the referee interfered, pulling on his own ear and making incoherent exclamations.

Benn landed a couple of good rights, and then swung a wild right hook that missed by a country mile. Again, the weight of the miss dragged his exhausted body forwards and took him to the canvas. This time though, Benn's forehead caught McClellan on the right eyebrow as he fell. It appeared no more than a glancing blow at first, but McClellan spiralled away in pain and removed his mouthpiece. He tapped at his own head, indicating to the referee that there had been a clash of heads. Suddenly, he sunk to one knee and began breathing heavily, clearly distressed. The crowd reacted to the drama by raising the volume even further. This was relentless excitement.

Significantly, WBC rules state that at this point the referee could have, and perhaps should have, called a five minute break from the action. This is to allow any injured fighter appropriate time to recover from that accidental foul – headbutts are particularly dangerous, for obvious reasons. A doctor at ringside could also have been given opportunity to examine the injured fighter and assess his ability to continue. In the event that the doctor had advised against the injured fighter resuming action, the fight would then have gone to the judges' scorecards to decide the winner. Both fighters would then have received any required medical attention, without having further injury inflicted. To consider this now sends a chill down my spine. 'What if's' are pointless.

Needless to say, Alfred Asaro did not take the above course of action. Instead, Mr Asaro gestured for McClellan to stand up and continue fighting. Though clearly distressed and uncomfortable, McClellan rose to his feet. He sucked in a hard, deep breath which exposed the ligaments of his neck. He allowed Asaro to reinsert his mouthpiece, and he boxed on towards his fate.

For what my own humble opinion is worth, I believe the referee made a fatal error here. I accept that referees must make vital decisions in a heartbeat and under intense pressure. I also believe that this referee made the wrong decision. Nevertheless, the fight was resumed. As battle recommenced, Jim Watt made what now sounds like a chilling statement: 'A big question mark hangs over McClellan now, Reg.'

Still visibly sucking in deep breaths, McClellan came bravely forwards. The fighters' heads brushed each other again. Benn struck McClellan with two more rabbit punches and again the referee waved ridiculing fingers at him. Benn again responded with a theatrical, apologetic bow. At ringside, Ferdie Pacheco voiced outrage: 'There's no point bowing if you just keep on committing the same foul.'

At the round's end, McClellan took to his stool blinking with both eyes. He sucked in more deep breaths as his corner team began working on him. When I watch this small section of footage now for the ten millionth time, I can't help wondering if the damage had been done there and then in that brief coming together of skulls. I can't help looking into Gerald's face and wondering in torment whether a great part of him was already slipping away into the abyss of tangled brain cables. The complex human mind is mere soft tissue, after all.

Round 10:

In Benn's corner, Dennie Mancini roared at his fighter, 'He half swallowed it that round. Three rounds to go and you'll be the champion of champions!'

However badly hurt he must have been, McClellan came out dancing. Switching tactics again, he stayed on the outside now and threw a few good jabs. But something wasn't right. McClellan was visibly blinking furiously and occasionally dabbing at his own face with his right glove. These were uncharacteristic mannerisms. In the unseen space behind his eyes, something was beginning to go seriously wrong.

The fighters grappled in Benn's corner, both exhausted, both fighting on instinct. Benn landed a decent right hand and then missed with two wild hooks. Nothing really connected. But suddenly McClellan sank to one knee. He wasn't knocked down, exactly. He just bent his knees suddenly and he slid downwards. He crouched there with one gloved hand resting high on his hip. He looked around himself with a puzzled expression. He was breathing quick, shallow breaths, his eyes blinking curiously. The London crowd went completely berserk around him. Lights flashed. Grown men screamed. Nobody in the world could help him now. It was Gerald against the world.

Somehow, he got up. McClellan was up at the count of six, but nothing about him suggested that he really wanted to carry on fighting. He stood in the corner looking tired and confused, a shadow of the confident warrior who had entered the ring just half an hour ago. He would not throw another single punch in this fight (or in any fight for that matter). Instead, he half-heartedly covered up and let Benn swarm him with one final attack. This was to be the end.

Benn threw another cluster of tired punches, ending with a short uppercut through the middle. None landed cleanly, none looked significant. But again McClellan went to one knee, sinking abruptly as if by choice. The crowd erupted again.

'He's going to stop him!' Reg Gutteridge gasped in disbelief.

'He's quit, Reg,' Jim Watt said, stunned. 'He's quit.'

'There's something wrong; what's making him go down like this?' Ring-doctor Pacheco puzzled.

Asaro picked up the count, in French of course: 'Un, Deux, Trois...' McClellan looked up at him as though looking straight through him, as though he could make no sense of what he was seeing. He stayed there on one knee, confusion and discomfort painfully clear on his face, a gloved hand rested almost effeminately on his hip, the loneliest man in the universe.

Benn's corner team mouthed along with each passing second. Don King's head was now just feet away from McClellan's on the other side of the ropes. Something like dismay appeared to draw his face into a scowl; hundreds of thousands of dollars were surely spilling through his bejewelled fingers. He screamed at Gerald to stand and fight. The order was ignored, if it was heard at all.

Frank Warren was just feet away, fists clenched with mounting excitement. Naz and Bruno were on their feet. An entire world watched with bated breath. No British fight fan wanted the American to get up. My Dad was on the edge of our couch, eyes wide in delirium. I was kneeling in front of our television, kneeling like Gerald, a twelve year old boy in pyjamas. Euphoria enveloped us. Lord forgive us, we could not possibly know...

'He's going to count him out, isn't he?' Reg Gutteridge half-asked half-stated in a fit of absolute shock and awe.

This time, McClellan stared down at the canvas. No longer the ferocious Alpha Male, no longer in control, he blinked rapidly. His cheeks rippled as he breathed hard, shallow breaths, that mouthpiece again sticking out clumsily. He let the referee's count reach 'Dix' and then instantly stood up. He walked back to his corner with his head down, defeated, a beaten man. The roof came off.

Standing in a neutral corner, the shattered Nigel Benn watched the battle come to its strange climax. He must have felt he was dreaming. He bent his knees in slow-motion and raised his fists in exhausted, relieved celebration. Just like that, it was over. It was really over. Pandemonium ensued.

'This ring is gonna be like the London underground at rush hour!' Reg Gutteridge said.

'This guy could now run for head of government!' Ferdie Pacheco said.

It was *really* over. The invading beast was defeated. The hometown underdog had done it. If the story ended there, it would have been almost perfect.

An impulsive, formidable release of euphoria exploded around the arena. Frank Warren and Prince Nazeem dived into the ring; Nigel Benn leapt into the arms of Kevin Sanderson and then bounded up the ring post to scream at the crowd. Security guards tried in vain to keep out the charging fans who stormed the ring just to touch and pat and congratulate the victorious champion. Jimmy Lennon

Junior fished for a microphone amid the growing tsunami of bodies. An attractive blonde girl jumped up onto the ring apron, suddenly enthralled and instantly addicted to this sweet, sweet chaos. A ring doctor and an anaesthetist scrambled through the ropes, oxygen tank and medical kit in hands, their faces strained with professional concern. Don King forced a smile and positioned himself tactfully next to the surprise winner. Gary Newbon and a cameraman grabbed their headsets and fought through the mass of people to interview the victor. Men in tuxedos and women in frocks and gowns cheered and cried and embraced perfect strangers with cathartic joy.

'I just never saw a fighter quit like that,' Ferdie Pacheco said in confusion (these words would later enrage members of the McClellan camp. He could not possibly have realised what he was saying). Pacheco too, grabbed a mic and fought his way towards the ring to interview whoever he could get near to.

'They only brought him over here to bash me up,' Nigel Benn scowled into a camera as fans surrounded him. 'Maybe now you'll start believing in the Dark Destroyer.'

'Well, you made a believer out of me!' Don King gushed sycophantically and forced a grin.

In a lonely corner of the ring, Gerald McClellan sat down on the canvas. Dehydrated, inert, battered, he blinked and breathed and looked around in a detached daze. Surely, he could make no sense of the chaos going on around him. The world was fading. Was this all for him?

Standing over him, Stan Johnson affectionately squirted water from a bottle onto his fighter's head. Gerald looked up at Stan in pained confusion.

'Damn,' Gerald said, 'that water you just poured on my head felt like it was running *inside* my head.'

Seconds later, Gerald laid his head against the bottom ring rope. He took another deep breath and then closed his eyes. Only a few bystanders seemed to grasp the seriousness of the situation. One cramped corner of the arena became a makeshift emergency room as the small medical team fought to revive Gerald. All around them, chaos reigned. Nigel Benn and his entourage celebrated without restraint. A minor fight broke out at the back of the crowd as adrenaline bubbled over and someone threw a chair. Already eyeing up his next big payday, Benn began calling out Roy Jones. Immediately reminding him who the decision maker was, Don King told him he'd have to fight Michael Nunn first. This is the fight business.

'This is crazy!' Ferdie Pacheco exclaimed. 'In one place it's jubilation; in the other it's total dejection.'

Jimmy Lennon Junior shouted over the microphone that people needed to clear the aisles urgently – an ambulance was required; its engine was already running in the carpark. For those close enough to realise what was going on, it was time to panic. For Gerald McClellan, it was the beginning of the fight of his life.

Hundreds of miles away in Illinois, Gerald's family did not yet know the outcome of the fight. His sisters, his children and his live-in girlfriend as yet had no clue. They did not yet know that their man had lost. They did not yet know that he was plummeting towards death. They had no idea that they would soon be hurrying to board a plane for England.

5

King Amongst Men

'Boxing is the only sport where you can get your brain shook, your money took and your name in the undertaker's book.' Joe Frazier, Boxing Legend

Lisa McClellan is not particularly fond of Don King. I have never met the man. What I do know is that an argument can present itself with the mere mention of his name.

Late one night, I was speaking to Ms McClellan on the phone about the financial details of my book. It was evening for her in Illinois; it was the small hours of the morning for me in England. Basically, my publisher had sent Lisa a draft contract at her behest and Lisa wasn't exactly thrilled with the stated terms. When she messaged me asking if I could call her, I was actually sitting drunk in a Manchester hotel room. I had spent the evening at a minor boxing dinner-do where an acquaintance of mine was making his professional debut. I had tagged along for something to do – my friend had won by a six round decision; I had spent the last four rounds sitting at the bar.

I called Lisa and she explained her issue with the contract. It was a minor misunderstanding, more to do with the wording than with the numbers, really. Trying to make light of the situation with my dry, English sense of humour, I quipped something along the lines of, 'Now I see how hard Don King had it dealing with you...'

It was a poor joke and it landed wider of the mark than would a left hand from Stevie Wonder (sorry). Still, it was meant in jest and delivered completely without malice. Unfortunately, Lisa didn't take it that way at all.

'Hell no!' she snapped in her fierce Illinoisan tongue. 'Now you're trying to piss me off.'

I apologised unreservedly and insisted it was an innocent, off-the-cuff remark. She wasn't pleased.

'You say you care about Gerald and what we've been through, and then you joke like that about Don King?' Lisa continued. 'That's no good, Wayne. If you knew how much I hate that man...'

I have been in the firing-line of angry women before – my kid's mum would make a good cruiserweight when she's in the mood, and my own mum once hit me with the best overhand right I've ever been caught with. But this was the first time I had ever been rebuked by an American woman (first, but not last). The accent definitely adds something to it. Maybe the knack for enraging females is universal. Either way, I had a sudden sense that this wasn't going to plan. The last thing I ever wanted to do was offend the McClellan family. What is it they say about 'no good deed'...?

In the beginning, I had never expected to form a friendship with Lisa McClellan. I had never expected to speak to her as often as I now do. My wildest hope in first contacting her had been to possibly gain a couple of interviews and maybe have her grant me access to a few other people in Gerald's closest circle. I wanted to get a firsthand insight into their lives over the past twenty-two years, possibly be privy to an update on Gerald's condition and, genuinely, to tell a story I have been fascinated by since I was just a wide-eyed twelve year old boxing fan. If I could send a few extra dollars Gerald's way in the process, then so much the better.

It was actually Lisa, in our very first telephone conversation, who had suggested we establish a contractual agreement to include her side of the story in this publication. I was aware that would undoubtedly lead to a very different book to the one I initially had in mind. But I am also very aware that writing is a fluid process - the best projects invariably evolve significantly between the embryonic concept and the finished article. Besides that, the thought of writing a book not just *about* one of my all time heroes, but actually *with* the closest of his kin, was almost enough to have me doing back-flips with delight. Some might say I'm easily pleased, but we all have our own life goals.

Now, with a minor contractual dispute and my stupid, pointless, not-even-funny reference to Don King, it looked like Lisa would be unwilling to deal with me on either version of the project. I had blown it in typical Wayne fashion.

'Do you think I'm just some dumb chick?' she asked me. 'People have taught me well over these years.'

I apologised some more and thought fleetingly about hanging myself with a hotel bed sheet. At least the attention would probably help my books sell a few extra copies. But I was being dramatic, of course. For every problem, there is a solution. This was all *so* minor.

Thankfully, after a few more sincere apologies on my part, Lisa composed herself. The conversation soon settled into a normal rhythm again. She told me her invitation to visit their family home in Freeport was still open. I told her I intended to fly out to Chicago this side of Christmas. I washed with relief at having her back on side, for now at least.

In the background, I could hear Gerald. I couldn't make out what he was saying exactly, but he sounded agitated. The babbling sound was constant, varying in volume and pitch. At one point, I thought I heard him say, 'God damn it, boy!' I wondered if my earlier, brief misunderstanding with his sister had somehow unsettled him. I hoped to God it hadn't.

When I asked if Gerald was OK and whether I had caused his apparent unrest, Lisa became sombre and replied, 'No; he doesn't even know we're talking right now. He just gets like this sometimes. It's difficult.'

My heart broke a little bit more for her. Staring into a telephone hundreds of miles away, I was getting the tiniest, most raw glimpse of what Lisa McClellan has had to live with, day in day out, night in night out, since 1995. The rest of us, those who call ourselves boxing fans, we really do not have a clue. There was so much I wanted to say to Lisa, but in my head it all sounded like platitudes and she must have heard enough of them to last her a lifetime.

For the remainder of that phone call, I had one ear on Gerald. I can still hear him now in a quiet corner of my mind; a sort of nonsensical, childlike muttering, like the mysterious words that leak from the dreams of a deeply worried man while he sleeps; slurred ramblings, interjected here and there by louder, random, high-pitched outbursts that might mean nothing or everything or something in between.

I listened hard, but the words meant nothing to me. I wondered what they meant to him, if they meant anything at all. I wondered what thoughts and images turn over in his lacerated and fragmented mind while he sits each day looking out at the murky world through eyes that cannot see. I wondered how much is really left of the G-Man; what really remains of that gladiator adorned in green and gold who stepped inside the ring that night and lifted his mighty fist towards the crowd; what remains of that slick and savage soldier of the ring, that confident young man so certain that this was just another night, another fight, another prelude to glory? Is he him? Is he really him? Or am I just obsessed with a living ghost, a twelve year old boy in a grown man's body, trying in vain to tell the story of a warrior who no longer exists?

When the phone call was over, I lay in the darkness of the hotel room. My mind was still far off in a small town of Illinois that my body had never set foot in. I closed my eyes and struggled to sleep for thoughts of Gerald McClellan, just as I had one night over twenty-two years ago.

Once upon a time, Don King was Gerald McClellan's manager and promoter. As our story progresses, it seems pertinent that we develop an understanding of the man and his background. All will become clearer as we go on, trust me.

Instantly recognisable the world over, the bombastic King has promoted fights for just about every big name in boxing from the mid 1970's up to the last decade – Ali, Holmes, Tyson, Duran, Chavez, Lewis – the list is endless. Over the past ten years, the emerging promotional outfits of Oscar De La Hoya's *Golden Boy* and Eddie Hearn's *Matchroom Sport* may have succeeded in finally loosening King's grip on the business. But as he approaches eighty-four years old with a multi-million dollar fortune in the bank, he probably doesn't lose much sleep over it.

The more research one undertakes into the man Don King, the more two ill-fitting facts present themselves: 1 - no boxing promoter has staged more million dollar grossing fights; 2 - no boxing promoter has had more lawsuits filed against him by the fighters he promoted. Clearly, King is a man of controversy, contradictions and cunning. As celebrated boxing journalist Jack Newfield once wrote, 'If Don King was a city, he would be Las Vegas: flamboyant, driven by money, rooted in gambling and the mob.'

In actual fact, King began his entrepreneurial ventures far from the bright lights and glamour of Nevada. Long before he came to dazzle the world with his electrified hair-do and outlandish suits, long before he baffled and beguiled his audience with phrases such as 'If the bullfrog had wings, he wouldn't bump his head every time he hopped,' King had cut his teeth as a mid-level street runner known as 'Donald the Kid.'

As a youth in the ghettos of Cleveland, the naturally driven and ruthless King had progressed quickly through the criminal ranks and made significant connections along the way. Initially working out of the basement of a friend's record store, the young Donald operated an illegal gambling and bookmaking business. By 'kicking up' a percentage of his illicit earnings to the Cleveland Mafia, King had involved himself early with heavyweight figures of organised crime. By his mid-twenties, he had already been arrested more than thirty times for demeanours ranging from gambling to assault.

In 1954, the twenty-three year old King was accosted again, this time for murder. King admitted to shooting dead a street rival named Hillary Brown, but claimed he had been acting in self-defence; the victim had been attempting to rob a gambling house which King controlled. Shockingly, even though Brown had been shot in the back, the killing was eventually deemed a justifiable homicide. King walked.

Thirteen years later in 1967, King claimed the life of another man. This time, he mercilessly kicked to death an employee named Sam Garrett in a dispute over the sum of $600. This second violent killing happened on a public street and even included a Cleveland police officer among its eye witnesses. For this felony, King was originally charged with second degree murder. Bizarrely, this sentence was also drastically reduced under suspicious circumstances. After a private meeting at which only King, his attorney and a district judge were present, second degree murder became manslaughter and King was soon a free man again. Even more remarkably, King was eventually pardoned of this crime all together.

Carl Delou, then of the Cleveland Homicide Unit, publically voiced suspicions over the motives behind the reduction of sentence: 'Why would that reduction of penalty from second degree murder to manslaughter happen on a Saturday morning and without the proper authorities being notified? It was a miscarriage of justice, there's no question about it.'

Regardless of the details, King had slipped the big shots yet again and managed to serve just four years in prison for brutally taking a man's life. In his own inimitable style, King later dismissed the whole saga as 'Frustrations of the ghetto expressing themselves.'

In the early 1970's, King began to spread his tentacles into the world of boxing. After learning of an Ohio hospital which was on the verge of closure due to financial pressures, the hawkeyed King saw an opportunity. He enlisted the help of an established local promoter named Don Elbaum and his rock singer acquaintance Lloyd Price to stage a major charity event. With savvy salesmanship, King managed to persuade ring legend of legends Muhammad Ali to play star attraction at the fundraiser. Up to this point, King and Ali had never actually met. But the cunning King appealed to Ali's proud racial sensitivities and convinced him that, as the hospital serviced a predominantly African American district, it was the duty of such a pillar of the black community as Ali to take action.

'When Don King started going into all of his "black solidarity" stuff, we would get hysterical,' Elbaum recalled dismissively. 'There got to be a point where Don would say "this is all bull shit. This is all crap. But whatever I got to do to sell it and get my point across, I'm going to sell it." He didn't care if you were white, black, or Chinese. He didn't care.'

Nevertheless, Ali was moved enough by King's spiel to offer his services. 'The Greatest' gladly boxed ten exhibition rounds against several sparring partners, putting on a typically mesmerising display full of showboating and foolery. The paying crowd of 8,500 people lapped it up. A fashion feature and pop concert completed the event and everyone went home happy. The hospital received a cheque for $20,000, and although unsubstantiated reports later suggested that not all of the money reached its intended recipient, Don King had found his foothold in pugilistic promotions. Just like a king, he had gone straight in at the top.

In 1973, King attended the world title fight between Joe Frazier and George Foreman in Jamaica. In a story which would come to typify King's shrewd stratagem, legend has it that he drove to the arena in the limousine of highly favoured champion Joe Frazier. But, when Frazier was promptly annihilated by the formidable young Foreman, King then travelled back from the arena in the backseat of Foreman's limo. The moral of the tale was this: Don King enters the arena with the champion and he leaves the arena with the champion, no matter what the outcome may be.

With his grip on the sport tightening, King landed a lucrative contract with the ABC Network to organise a televised boxing tournament. As ever, controversy was not far behind. The tournament was cut short amid rumours of match fixing and claims that the records of certain contenders had been doctored in order to benefit King-managed fighters. Scandal, treachery and illusion were becoming synonymous with Don King. The faster he talked, the more he dazzled and beguiled his paying audience. The more he lied and hyperbolised, the taller his grey crown grew.

'King's hair, his clothes, his jewellery, his lingo,' Seth Abraham, former CEO of HBO Sports once said, 'it's all an act. It's to confuse, it's to obscure, it's to disarm people.'

It seemed that King did not discriminate when it came to confusing and then short-changing his associates. As the career of the great Muhammad Ali came to its sad end and 'The Greatest' deteriorated with Parkinson's Disease, King took the opportunity of ripping off the man who had given him his start in the sport. Ali filed a $1 million lawsuit against King claiming he had not been paid for his final championship fight. At the time, Ali was struggling financially and had been hospitalised by the onset of his illness. Still, King had no intention of giving the revered champion his dues. Instead, King persuaded Ali's friend and fellow Muslim, Jeramiah Shabbazz, to intervene.

'I was in Don's office and Don gave me the money with specific instructions that I was not to give Ali the money unless he signed a release,' Shabbaz revealed. 'It was $50,000 cash.'

Shabbazz visited Ali in hospital and presented him with the case of money. Despite the sum being a mere fraction of what Ali was actually owed, the ailing champ was desperate enough to sign the release papers. King was off the hook again. To his credit, the middle-man Shabbaz later spoke of his regret at aiding the shady transaction.

'Don just uses people,' he stated. 'He just uses you up until he has no more use for you and then he moves onto the next one.'

'I'll always survive because I have the right mix of wit, grit and bullshit,' King once boasted. 'If you cast bread upon the water and have faith, you'll get back cash. If you don't have faith, you'll get soggy bread.'

By the 1980's, King wasn't worrying about soggy bread. Becoming as famous as the fighters he represented, King had established a monopoly on champions. He had also devised the most ingenious means of maintaining complete control over the fight game. Fundamentally, King saw to it that he and his step-son, Carl King, would hold the managerial reigns of both the champion and the challenger in all major title fights. That way no matter who the winner was, King still finished the night representing the champ. Some might call that a conflict of interests. Others might say it was completely unscrupulous. King, however, simply called it 'the American way.'

One of King's most vocal critics of this period was former world heavyweight champion, Tim Witherspoon.

'I began to feel King's presence from around my twelfth or thirteenth professional fight,' Tim explained. 'Every time I fought, he was in the crowd hollering out, "Ter-rible Tim! Ter-rible Tim! We gon' be alright!"'

Witherspoon went on to recount a horror story of how his once promising career was ruined by the Kings' greed and manipulation. The Philadelphian fighter claimed that King used his influence to have his boxing licence temporarily suspended. This meant that Witherspoon could not progress or even earn a living until he agreed to sign a promotional contract with Don. Reluctantly, the demoralised Tim finally agreed to sign. However, he alleges that he was then forced to sign three different contracts. The first contract gave King the standard thirty-three percent manager's fee. This one was filed with the State Athletic Committee to make all appear above board. The second 'illegal' contract awarded King an extortionate fifty percent. The third was a completely blank piece of paper to be abused at King's leisure. Effectively, Don King and his step-son would make more money from Tim's blood, sweat and tears than he would.

Despite winning the world heavyweight title twice, Witherspoon never became financially secure. Crazily, he was paid just $90,000 for his 1984 world title defence against Frank Bruno in London. For the same fight, one which generated many millions of dollars worldwide, the challenger was paid around $900,000 – ten times Witherspoon's purse. This sounds even more lubricious when you consider that Witherspoon knocked Bruno out!

'I was pulling mothballs out of my pockets,' Tim said, almost laughing at the absurdity of it all; a definite 'laugh or cry' situation.

When he finally reached his breaking point, Witherspoon filed a $25 million lawsuit against the Kings for fraud and loss of earnings. In response, the irrepressible King banned Tim from fighting any other boxer he promoted. This effectively meant that Witherspoon could not fight any top ten rated contender. Naturally, this would be sufficient to stifle and stall his career further. As the lawsuit began, Tim also alleges that he received serious threats against his own safety.

'[King] has a lot of money and money is power. I think we all know what can come after that...I have gone as far as arming myself for protection,' Witherspoon confessed.

Witherspoon's next manager, his long-time friend Tom Moran, confirmed the severity of the danger his man was in: 'Tim was told that if he didn't settle the lawsuit he wouldn't have to worry about settling lawsuits because he wouldn't be breathing,' he said.

Such revelations read like something out of a gangster movie. Perhaps it is no surprise then that in the 1980's, King was subject to a four year FBI investigation into his rumoured ties with organised crime. Like a storyline from *The Sopranos*, there were secret tape recordings, private liaisons with informants, wiretaps and surveillance. It was even believed but never proved beyond doubt that King had connections to infamous underworld Godfathers, John Gotti and Paul Castellano. An undercover FBI agent named Victor Quintana claimed that, whilst posing as a drug baron looking to launder money through professional boxing, he was led into a meeting with King by a high-ranking member of the notorious Genovese crime family.

As reported by Sports Illustrated at the time, 'These people were looking to launder illicit cash – to run their gains from gambling, thievery and the like, through the spin cycle of some legitimate enterprise so they could pull them out later, clean and fresh, and declare the money as earned income...Boxing, of all the sports, was perhaps the most accommodating Laundromat, what with its subculture of unsavoury characters who play by their own rules...I believed that King was involved with the wiseguys.'

Evidence against King seemed plentiful. In the end though, the allegations of intimidation and racketeering failed to stick. Most witnesses decided not to testify. Another key witness, a renowned boxing coach who claimed to have been threatened with death, retracted his statement altogether. Even when King *was* eventually indicted for the lesser charge of tax evasion, he again somehow slipped the punch. When he was eventually acquitted of all charges, King made a typically outlandish gesture of gratitude; he flew the entire jury out to London to watch a championship fight. This was the man. It seemed that even the FBI could not nail him.

'Don King is just a slimy, reptilian motherfucker,' Mike Tyson once said of his former promoter. 'He would kill his own mother for a dollar.'

Tyson, like Witherspoon, claims that he was robbed and misled by Don at every turn during his own turbulent career. Despite being the youngest world heavyweight champion of all time, the biggest grossing athlete throughout the 1990's and an idol to fight fans across the globe to this day, Mike too finished his career living pay cheque to pay cheque.

'Don doesn't know how to love anybody,' Tyson added poignantly.

Don King: this was the man.

Taking all of the above into account, it seems fair to assess Don King as a slippery and dangerous individual. Certainly, he is not the type of man one would wish to be on the wrong side of. Certainly, he is not the type of man one would wish to be on the wrong side of whilst trapped somewhere between life and death, unconscious on a life support machine, a vision of vulnerability...

In the early hours of a February morning, Don King arrived at a London hospital. He was no longer wearing that salesman smile, no longer waving plastic star-spangled-banners. It seemed his latest plan towards world domination was in tatters. He might now have been unwinding at a post-fight party, sipping champagne with his entourage, watching pretty girls pose for pictures with that garish but glorious green and gold belt. But something had gone wrong, hadn't it?

King left his minders in the waiting room and made his way into the Intensive Care Unit. Heart monitors beeped, respirators gasped and sighed. Stan and Donnie were already there, keeping a silent and sombre vigil over their friend. Don King stood at the foot of the bed and looked down at his failed investment with a grim frown. Gerald McClellan lay broken and bandaged. He was no longer aware of his surroundings, no longer a dangerous man, no longer a contender. He was simply a patient in critical condition. The doctors were unwilling or unable to promise that he would even survive the night.

Don King shook his head. Was he looking down at an injured young fighter? Was he looking down at millions of dollars in projected future earnings shredded into non-existence? Or, was he looking down at something else? There would be no more big paydays from this one. There might well be medical bills instead. King turned to face Stan Johnson.

'Gerald quit, man,' Don said. 'He quit like a dog.'

This was the man.

This was the man the McClellan family were counting on through that cold, dark February of 1995. This was the man holding the purse-strings to the family's future as their son and brother lay covered in tubes with stitches holding together his brain.

This was the man.

6

A Girl Named Maria

'Good guys don't make it in this game.' Gerald McClellan, 1994.

'What I am about to tell you, Wayne, I have never told anyone before in over twenty-two years,' Lisa began. Her tone was measured, precise. It was late and I was tired, but my pulse quickened with interest. 'No reporter or writer has ever been told this by me.'

'Go on,' I said, pulling the receiver closer to my eager ear.

'Gerald was having an affair,' Lisa continued. 'At the time of the Benn fight, he was having an affair with a girl named Maria Russey. She was a very attractive Puerto Rican girl and she worked for Don King, in one of his offices.'

'OK,' I said.

'But the thing is, Wayne, she was also Don King's girlfriend...'

I sat up in my chair. Now this was gripping stuff; a world exclusive; a bombshell. The story was becoming a Shakespearean drama.

'No way!' I gasped.

'Yes,' Lisa confirmed. She paused as if to let me digest this revelation and compute its many ramifications. 'You see, people don't realise, but female employees of Don King basically have it in their contracts that they have to be available to him sexually. That's just the kind of man he is.'

'This is unbelievable!' I said. My mind was racing with it.

'But Don must have cared somewhat about this one girl,' Lisa explained, 'because he was taking care of her family in Puerto Rico financially.'

'So she was more than just a side-piece?' I said.

'Exactly,' Lisa said. 'And she had fallen in love with Gerald.'

'And Don knew about this?' I guessed out loud.

'Don knew all about it and he wasn't happy,' Lisa confirmed. 'But the whole time Gerald was in London for the Benn fight, Maria was staying with Gerald in his hotel room.'

'Do you think Gerald loved her?' I ventured. My pen-hand was scribbling furious notes on my pad.

'I know he loved her,' Lisa replied ardently. There was no shred of doubt in her voice.

'So Gerald McClellan, the champ who could have any woman he wanted, went and fell in love with the mistress of Don King, the most powerful man in boxing?' I laid it all out flat.

'Yes,' Lisa confirmed simply.

I was wide awake now. This story was developing into something like a soap opera with boxing. The gangster, the gangster's moll and the handsome young fighter, her forbidden lover, the 'KO Kid' now languishing on a life support machine, and all this with the world's press baying at the door of the ward. This was some situation, a situation complicated further by Gerald's concurrent relationship with live-in girlfriend Angela Brown. Angie is the mother of his only daughter and was presently boarding a plane to London to be at her man's bedside – this was something straight from a Hollywood script and I was breaking the story firsthand from my living room in West Yorkshire. I couldn't sit still again.

Suddenly, pieces of a jigsaw were falling into place; things I had puzzled over all the years I had spent studying articles on the McClellans' story. It had never quite made sense to me that Lisa had flown Gerald back to the United States so soon after his life-saving brain surgery. Why had she taken such a risk with her brother's life? Why make that decision, against doctors' orders, knowing that a fifteen hour transatlantic flight in a special aircraft could finish him off?

'I had to get Gerald away from Don King,' Lisa said this slowly, emphasising each crucial word. 'Don King was controlling everything in London. He was the one speaking to the doctors. He was the one in charge of everything. He wanted to keep Gerald in London. I wanted to get my brother away from that man. I just wanted him home.' There was another pause on the line. 'I just wanted him home,' she said again.

'This is unbelievable,' I said.

'I told you,' Lisa replied, 'I have never told this to anyone outside of the family before.'

'I'm very grateful,' I assured her. If I could have hugged her down the phone I would have. All of our silly misunderstandings before now had been worth it.

'Did Gerald and Don ever have a confrontation about the Maria situation?' I asked.

'All the time,' she answered.

My mind was swimming with intrigue. My imagination served up a scenario of Don first introducing Maria to Gerald; King sitting at his desk in a plush office suite in New York or Florida, perhaps; King smoking an evil looking cigar, a designer suit failing to disguise his portly bulk; King flashing that slimy smile, the one that usually means somebody is about to get fucked, physically or figuratively; the handsome young fighter sitting opposite him, tall and lean, a thin moustache riding his top lip; the pretty Puerto Rican office girl hovering nearby, paperwork in hands, stealing glances at the champ; forbidden fruit is delicious. Soon it would all turn sour; soon the young fighter would be in a hospital bed and at this man's mercy.

'So,' Lisa continued the story, 'I kept on demanding that they fly Gerald back to the States until Don agreed. It was against Don's wishes and against the doctors' wishes, but I have no regrets. I would do it all again in a heartbeat.'

I asked if Lisa had not been afraid of flying her brother so far whilst in such a vulnerable state.

'Of course I was afraid,' she admitted. 'But it was a special aircraft and we had a surgeon on board who was prepared to perform surgery on Gerald at any time if it was needed. The worry was that, due to the air pressure when flying, they thought that could cause his brain to swell. But we had the surgeon on board and it was just a risk I had to take. That's how much I needed to get him out of there.'

I needed to know what happened next.

'Gerald never fully regained consciousness in England,' Lisa went on.

This surprised me, as it runs contrary to every news report and article I have ever read about the G-Man. Every report I have ever seen states that he regained consciousness after twelve days in a coma. I explained this to Lisa.

'No, that's not true,' Lisa asserted. 'His situation may have improved some, he may even have opened his eyes very briefly, but he was still in a comatose state the whole time we were in London.'

It just goes to show, don't believe everything you read.

'Don just wanted to keep him in London,' Lisa moved on. 'Eventually, I went to the American Embassy and told them I wanted him home. When Don finally agreed to fly Gerald back out to the States, it was now the April of '95. He arranged for him to be admitted to a hospital in Ann Arbour, Michigan. That again was Don's decision. I agreed with it just to get Gerald back to the States. The plane journey cost $99,000. To be at this hospital was costing $2,000 a day and we were there for four or five days and they did nothing. As far as I could see, they did nothing.'

'And Don was still making the decisions?' I said.

'Yes. So then, I had Gerald moved to a Coma Recovery Program in Milwaukee without Don knowing,' Lisa was free-flowing the events now, revealing things she has probably held in for years, perhaps even reliving it in her mind. 'That is not exactly close to where we live. But at the time our dad was living in Milwaukee, so it was the next best thing. So now, Don didn't know where Gerald was. I have never told anyone this before, Wayne, but I even had Gerald put in the hospital under a fake name. That's how much I did not want Don to find him.'

I felt honoured to be privy to this information. I hung on Lisa's every word. My imagination was in the hospital room with her; I could almost smell the disinfectant, hear the bleeps of monitors, see the family gathered in angst around the unconscious champ's bed, praying day and night for a miracle, a sign of sentient life. I was there.

I needed to know where the money was coming from to pay for this care. The Americans, for all of their great advances, do not have an NHS style system in place. Medical bills can therefore be astronomical. Even in life or death situations, there had better be a cheque book or insurance policy in place, or someone will be meeting their maker. Money talks. Land of the free, indeed! Obviously, as the Mid-West winter thawed into spring, somebody was paying for every breath Gerald took.

'Gerald still had some money banked from his previous fights,' Lisa said. 'That covered some of it.'

I explained to Lisa briefly what my extensive research had told me of the financial situation... In a nutshell, King claims that he paid for McClellan's medical bills in full. He even publically produced receipts amounting to $226,798. This included fees for Gerald's transport in the air ambulance and for his stay at Ann Arbour. There had been a standard insurance policy in place on the fight whereby the WBC would pay out $100,000 in the event of either fighter suffering a career ending injury. That sum wouldn't go very far. In fact, it would barely get the air ambulance from runway to runway.

I had struggled to make sense of all this over many lonely days and nights of research prior to first contacting Lisa. Now, with this 'Maria girl love triangle' thrown into the mix, it made even less sense. If Don King really is the bad guy that popular culture makes him out to be, if he really is the heartless crook and Mafioso that even justice runs scared of, would he really be paying out of his own funds to keep alive the vanquished young fighter who had so humiliated him by fucking his woman? Not only by fucking her, but by making her fall in love with him? Surely, an Alpha Male like Don King cannot afford to be cuckolded so spectacularly. Imagine the snide comments in the gyms he governed, the sniggers behind his back in his offices. What would his business partners say? What would John Gotti say?

'There was a second insurance policy that I found out about,' Lisa said with a shrewdness sneaking into her tone. 'I asked a lot of questions and I found out myself. Don had taken out a second insurance policy with the BBBC (British Boxing Board of Control). This was worth $250,000 and Don was the beneficiary. They paid him out.'

This plot just kept on thickening. I let myself drown in it like quicksand.

'So, you're saying that any money Don gave towards Gerald's care wasn't out of his own pocket?' I said, trying to get my head around it. 'It was basically from Gerald's own insurance money?'

'Basically, yes,' Lisa said. 'Ethically, it was Gerald's. But legally, Don was the beneficiary.'

This was incredible. My ears were wide open. The story was twisting and turning and this was only the beginning of a furious feud which would escalate all the way up to the offices of the FBI (more on that later).

I told Lisa about another story I had heard whilst digging around. I had been told that Don King had had his goons steal Gerald's copy of the contract for the Benn fight from Gerald's London hotel room whilst the fighter was still in a coma. My understanding had been that this was done so that King could run a phony contract on the McClellans, thus giving himself a bigger cut of the purse. Lisa surprised me here by not taking an obvious opportunity to make more accusations.

'It wasn't just the contract that was removed from the room,' Lisa admitted. 'The thing was, Gerald's girlfriend Angie was flying out to be with him in the hospital. So, Don's men went to remove all of Maria's things from the hotel room before Angie got there. That was the reason they went to the hotel room. We never had the contract again after that, so we said it could have been taken from the hotel room then.'

Of course, there is no proof that such a theft ever took place, however warranted the family's suspicions may seem when all is taken into account. Ultimately, King refused all requests to provide copies of the contract to any news organizations or to the McClellan family. He also vehemently denied that it mysteriously vanished after the fight.

'The contract was never lost,' King said. 'It's here. It is what it says it is - $200,000 plus $50,000 for training expenses.'

When I asked Lisa if she ever formally mounted a lawsuit against the Kings to pursue the amount they believed missing, the answer was painful to hear: 'No one would take a case against him. Nor did we have the money [to fund a trial].'

Two men who *were* in a position to chase King for monies owed to them were John Davimos and Emanuel Steward. Davimos had been Gerald's manager and Steward his trainer. They had split from the champ on unpleasant terms prior to the Benn fight. Complicating the situation further, they claimed that McClellan still owed them $119,000 for their work in his previous fights.

'Gerald told me Don King was going to pay the $119,000,' Davimos said. 'Two days before the Benn fight, I got a cheque from Don King Productions for $119,000. Immediately after the fight, Don King stopped payment on the cheque. I said, "No chance. You made a deal with Gerald. I'll force the judgment." King said, "Gerald is in this situation; you can't take the money." I told Don I'd pick my own charities. Who knew he was going to take it out of Gerald's purse?'

King admitted that he did ask Davimos and Steward not to take the money, saying, 'These two guys are so cold-blooded they didn't give the McClellans a dime.' But he outright denied Lisa's claim that he ever promised to pay the $119,000 judgment.

By the end of this phone conversation, my head was crammed. Between all of the claims and counter-claims, sandwiched between the ugliness of Don King's dealings and the McClellans' suffering, all I could think about was exactly how much Gerald had really lost that night. The more I read, the more I heard, the more my amazement grew at exactly how much a man can lose in a fight lasting all of thirty minutes: health, money, security, a dream of true love. God, Gerald, that was some defeat.

'Some time later,' Lisa carried on, 'Maria contacted us and said that she just wanted us to know that she really loved Gerald. But Don King had forbidden her from ever contacting our family again.'

To me, that seemed like one last vicious twist of the knife.

'Does Gerald ever mention her to this day?' I wondered out loud. Even the Romantic in me wouldn't have expected it to be so.

'Yes, from time to time he talks about her,' Lisa shocked me again. 'Nothing big; he'll just bring her up.'

It really must have been love, I thought. Maria is still in there. She is still tangled up somewhere in his fractured mind. She is still in his heart.

'Lisa,' I said. 'Let's find her.'

Lisa answered, fearlessly as always, 'We can try.'

7

The Morning After the Fight Before

'I was trying to push the nose bone up into the brain.' Mike Tyson after breaking Jesse Ferguson's nose with an uppercut, 1985.

'He has suffered a clot on the brain which will certainly end his career and *will* kill him if he doesn't have surgery,' Doctor John Sutcliffe addressed the assembled media from a small desk in a room at the Royal London Hospital. His tone was matter-of-fact, bordering on blunt.

Somewhere down the hall, Gerald McClellan was lying unconscious with pen markings on his freshly shaven scalp. He was prepped for theatre, waiting to have a scalpel open up his skull, but he was of course oblivious to that fact.

Doctor Sutcliffe MD – MBcHB FRCS (SN), is a neurosurgeon and master of his trade. He was also no stranger to this type of tragic situation. On the 26th April 1994, just ten months prior to the Benn Vs McClellan fight, Dr Sutcliffe had operated on another young fighter. British super-bantamweight contender Bradley Stone had been rushed into the exact same hospital with a near identical injury to the one which now had Gerald's life hanging in the balance. The similarities were chilling – a subdural haematoma, which in layman's terms constitutes a clotting of blood between the inside of the skull and the surface of the brain. Horrifically, young Bradley had collapsed at his girlfriend's house some hours after losing his British title challenge by a tenth round stoppage – it had even been the same round that Gerald was stopped in. Dr Sutcliffe had performed a two hour operation on Bradley's brain that night before addressing the gathered press.

'After the operation to remove the blood clot, a follow up scan showed that the brain was swollen, and that the blood supply to the left and some of the right side was inadequate for some time...Some parts of the brain were dead or dying.'

There had been no happy ending here. On the 28th April, Bradley Stone's life support machine had been switched off. He was just twenty-four years old. A statue was later erected in Bradley's honour outside the Peacock Gym in London. On it, the inscription read, 'A brave young man who died in pursuit of his dreams.'

Gerald McClellan, of course, had finalised his training preparations at that very same gym. He had passed that statue every single day during his stay in London. Eerily, Gerald had even paused at the statue just days before the Benn fight. He had turned to his coach Stan Johnson and said, 'Man, that will never happen to me...'

Here, Dr John Sutcliffe found himself again, with the life of a young fighter literally resting in his skilled hands. If those hands were to tremble with nerves at all, few could have blamed him. Somehow though, he appeared professionally composed as the questions and camera flashes of the world's press rained over him.

'His blood clot is exactly similar,' the good doctor said, referring to the matching injuries of poor Bradley and poor Gerald. 'The advantage that Gerald has is that he got here quicker than Bradley did. And that his resuscitation, such as was required, was more complete in that he was oxygenated from the time he went down in the corner immediately after the fight was stopped...It is, in fact, still too early to say whether or not he is going to survive this blood clot. But things look promising in that sense.'

Soon after delivering this impromptu press conference, Dr Sutcliffe performed a three and a half hour operation on Gerald's brain. He succeeded in removing the clot, releasing the great build up of pressure inside Gerald's skull and bringing at least a part of him back from the brink of certain death. In that respect, it might be said that some shred of something close to a positive outcome had been salvaged this time around.

By morning though, follow up tests brought more terrifying news. Results indicated that Gerald had suffered two strokes in the immediate aftermath of his collapse. It seemed very possible that he had also suffered a cardiac arrest – the brain controls everything. His condition was still critical. Besieged by such a merciless onslaught of severe physical ailments all at once, it became increasingly likely that if Gerald did pull through, he would never be the same man again.

As Gerald lay unconscious and oblivious in a post-op recovery bay, another fight had broken out around him. This time, it was a battle between the sport of boxing and those who opposed its existence as a legal activity. The British Medical Association, apparently appalled at the ferocity of the fight and by the fact that another young man now lay irreparably damaged, led fresh and furious calls for boxing to be outlawed altogether.

Dr Fleur Fisher, Head of Ethics and Science at the British Medical Association, was immediately at the forefront of the attack on pugilism.

'What the BMA would like to do is tear up the rule book and throw it away and say that boxing is no longer considered a sport and should be banned in the UK,' Ms Fisher declared without restraint.

This stance was backed up by another neurosurgeon, Dr Peter Hamlyn. He stated, 'The boxers now are better athletes than they have ever been, they can deliver a harder punch than they have ever been able to, but the brain they are boxing with is just as delicate as it's been since the beginning of time.'

Boxing was quick to defend itself though. Frank Warren, the joint promoter of the ill-fated showdown, was swarmed by reporters on his arrival at the hospital. He dismissed suggestions that his sport should be banned as 'knee jerk reactions.'

'I don't think the BMA should moralise,' Warren said later. 'They should feel free to talk to boxers about the risks. But I don't think they should moralise and decide on freedom of choice and what people want to do.'

One doctor who agreed with Warren was Dr Adrian Whiteson, of the British Boxing Board of Control. He pointed out that banning boxing would present its own problems: 'One thing we will not be doing is agreeing that we should ban it. Because all you do then is drive it underground and then these types of things will occur and there'll be no support whatsoever.'

The anti-boxing brigade countered such claims by insisting that if an outright ban could not be agreed, then massive changes should be made to the sport to limit the damage fighters may suffer. Suggested alterations included - removing the head as a target area for punches, making only body contact legal, making boxing gloves bigger and softer to emphasise protection of the head rather than of the hands, making professional fighters wear protective headgear in all contests, reducing the number of rounds, shortening the length of rounds, increasing the interval between rounds, bringing weigh-ins further away from the date of the fight to allow more time for fighters to rehydrate themselves after sacrificing their diet to make weight, and even having doctors check combatants for signs of brain injury between each and every round of every fight.

Naturally, such ideas failed to breach boxing's defences. When some boxing experts began pointing out that, statistically, boxing was still safer than many other ostensibly 'tamer' pastimes, the detractors brushed them off. Factually, in the decade leading up to the Benn Vs McClellan fight, there had been only two known deaths in boxing. This number, although tragic, paled in comparison to a surprising nine in cricket and a shocking *ninety-four* in horse riding.

'Success in boxing is causing acute brain damage by inflicting a knockout,' Dr Fleur Fisher hit back. Her suggestion here was that although injuries may occur in other sports, they tend to occur through accident rather than intent. Even with that being the case, one might presume that *ninety-four* fatalities from a 'sport' - one which involves lightweight men violently whipping a powerfully built animal - might suffice to have doctors such as Ms Fisher aiming their professional contempt in that direction. On the contrary, boxing remained top of the hit-list for such critics.

'We can no longer go on watching two men inflicting brain damage upon themselves and having audiences pay large sums of money to cheer this on,' Sam Galbraith, a Labour MP, joined the debate in favour of a proposed blanket banning. Politicians can be trusted to catch a bandwagon, if with nothing else.

In the wake of all this controversy, the ITV television network had resisted the temptation to show reruns of the Benn-McClellan fight coverage. Despite immense public interest, it had seemed in poor taste to air repeats while one of the combatants was still not out of the woods.

Just one week after the fight, ITV did screen the latest bout of emerging featherweight spectacle, Prince Naseem Hamed. Flashy Naz, who had been such a vocal spectator at the Benn fight, scored a spectacular knockout of Sergio Liendo of Argentina. Hard hitting Hamed landed a devastating left hook that left the Argentine's head bouncing off the canvas and his eyes rolling back into his skull. Ringside spectators gasped 'Not again!' whilst commentator Jim Watt lamented, 'This is the last thing we needed tonight.'

With no sense of irony, Naz had turned towards television cameras and affectionately dedicated the victory to Gerald McClellan, even as ring-doctors were simultaneously peeling Liendo off the canvas. Thankfully, Liendo made a quick and full recovery. Still, the violent finish only gave critics more ammunition – another reason to say boxing is barbaric. With that, ITV removed boxing from its roster. It would be ten whole years before they screened a live fight again.

The arguments for and against a boxing ban would continue to rage on for many weeks and months. All the while, Gerald lay prone in his hospital bed. He slept in solitary depths with his head wrapped in gauze, completely unaware of the ensuing war that he was at the dead-centre of. In his lacerated mind it might now forever be the 25th February 1995.

Just a few hours after they had stood toe-to-toe as professional enemies, two fighters were briefly reunited. Both were badly damaged, one worse than the other.

Nigel Benn, the victorious retaining champion, probably didn't look much like a winner. He was battered and bruised. A routine scan revealed that a worrying shadow had formed on his brain. His right cheekbone was badly damaged and he would be urinating blood for several days due to the hammer his kidneys had taken. Still, at least he was conscious. His brief passing out in the dressing room after the fight had most likely been the result of fatigue. He was awake now, sitting in a wheelchair, but only as a precaution. He'd live to fight another day.

The 'Dark Destroyer', sitting in his temporary, precautionary wheelchair, a large bandage fastened to his face, a green and gold championship belt sitting in a bag with the rest of his belongings, a cheque for 700,000 English pounds waiting to clear in his bank account, wanted to see somebody; he wanted to see Gerald McClellan.

Soon, Benn was wheeled into the cubicle where Gerald lay unconscious. Stan Johnson and Donnie Pendleton stood by their man, both settling in for a long night. God only knew what the morning would bring. Nigel, now the gracious and compassionate winner, claims that he took Gerald's limp hand in his, the same hand which just hours ago had been a proficient tool employed to crush him. He kissed that hand softly and said simply, 'I'm sorry.'

This paints images of a sweet and painfully tender moment; professional rivals reduced to men; trained soldiers restored to humanity once the war is over. Given the circumstances, 'I'm sorry,' was probably all that Benn could have said in that most poignant and private moment. It was probably all that needed to be said.

In the morning though, with all the cameras and all the eyes of the world once again trained upon him, Nigel, the gracious and compassionate, would say something else. This time, it was something that definitely did not need to be said.

'Rather him than me,' was Nigel's response when a journalist asked how he felt about Gerald's condition. A swarm of reporters had waited patiently for the champion to make his exit from the hospital. The cold-hearted remark smacked of misjudged insensitivity at best, disgraceful contempt at worst. Nevertheless, it was what it was. Benn was cleared to leave the hospital and Gerald wasn't. Benn was back in his civilian clothes of jeans, hoody and hat and Gerald wasn't. Nigel Benn was going back home to his family in one piece, and Gerald McClellan wasn't.

Leaning against a wall bearing a *No Smoking* sign, Stan Johnson sucked greedily on a cigarette. His face was strained from lack of sleep and from the angst of his world crumbling around him. His trademark pilot's cap was still in place on his head. If he had a pilot's licence to go with it, he might well have thought about flying himself back home to Illinois. It wasn't turning out very nice here in England.

In between sitting in wait at Gerald's bedside and making phone calls back home to the champ's distraught relatives in the States, Stan leaned in this small shelter by the automatic doors of the hospital ward and smoked his cigarettes. Each time he came out, journalists pounced with their cameras and questions. They wanted to know how Gerald was doing, they wanted to know what had gone wrong, they wanted to know who was to blame for this tragedy. Stan Johnson, the coach with his front teeth missing – the result, he claims, of an intentional, playful punch in the mouth his homeboy Gerald had once whacked him with during a gym session - didn't mince his words. He knew exactly what had gone wrong and he knew exactly who was to blame.

'That fool, who could not ref a dog fight of mine, did no such thing,' Stan growled when asked whether the fight should have been stopped far earlier than it was. 'So the fight goes ten rounds, my guy ends up in a coma, and why? Because of a stupid-ass referee!'

With that, Johnson extinguished his cigarette, turned on his heels and marched back through the sliding doors of the hospital. And with that, the tabloids had another headline, another angle from which to attack this fast evolving story – the coach blamed the referee. But Stan's offence in the name of self-defence had inadvertently begged another question: if he really thought the fight should have been stopped before the tenth, then why didn't he, in his capacity of chief corner-man, stop it? That very question would eventually be referee Asaro's lead-counter when it was his turn to face the world's press.

'It's my job to make a guy get up and wreak havoc in the other guy's corner,' Johnson would later hit back in Asaro's direction, 'it's your job to stop fights.'

Such a strong retort might sound assertive. It also sounds like a gross misunderstanding of the full duties of a chief second. Wreaking havoc is all well and good. Sending your man back out to fight when you sense he is no longer capable might be bordering on incompetency. I couldn't help but wonder which of these two characters Lisa held responsible, if any.

'Both,' Lisa answered me without hesitation. 'When Gerald was blinking and his mouthpiece wouldn't stay in right, that should have been a sign that something was wrong. Both men were in a position to stop the fight, so I blame both.'

You can always rely on Lisa for a straight answer.

'But blaming people now won't change anything,' she adds pragmatically. She was correct again.

So, February 26th 1995, the morning after the fight before; Nigel Benn was safely home. Gerald McClellan was lost in space. The media were out in force. The coach blamed the referee. The referee blamed the coach. The BMA blamed boxing itself. Meanwhile, somewhere in Detroit, Michigan, a wily old boxing genius was contemplating blaming himself.

As he fought back tears and waited anxiously for news from London, the great Emanuel Steward, the coach who had been Gerald's mentor and father figure, the coach who had guided him to two world titles, the coach who had left his side on unpleasant terms just a few fights ago, now had variations of one big question burning in his wisdom-crammed mind: what if I'd been there? What if I was still in Gerald's corner? What if...

8

Emanuel

'Training fighters is like catching a fish; it's technique, not strength.' Angelo Dundee, Coach

'Gerald and Emanuel had a relationship exactly like father and son,' Lisa told me one night. 'When Gerald became champion, his ego exploded. He wanted people around him who would do whatever he say. So he left Manny and brought in Stan Johnson...I'm telling you now, if Gerald had taken a shit in the middle of the gym and told Stan Johnson to pick it up with his bare hands, he would have done it without question.'

Lisa's honesty was as direct and razor sharp as always. I sat with the phone to my ear, my pen scribbling notes on a pad.

I had long since been intrigued by the break up between Gerald and his former Kronk mentor, Emanuel Steward. The unfortunate split is perhaps reminiscent of Mike Tyson being lured away from his formative stable of Cus D'Amato/Kevin Rooney by the lecherous Don King in the late 1980's (do you see a pattern emerging?). Tyson had been transformed from a lost soul and juvenile street mugger, into a disciplined and adored fighting machine whilst learning at the knee of his adoptive father, Cus. After Cus passed away and young Mike walked out on what remained of the close-knit camp - the camp that had guided him to unprecedented glory at age twenty - he had forged a chaotic path of self-destruction. He had surrounded himself with 'Yes men' and hangers-on who really never had his best interests at heart. Before long, he had thrown his once promising legacy into the fire and replaced it with one of bitten ears, disgraceful losses, rape cases and prison sentences. It is a spectacularly sad story of what might have been, and I wondered how closely it had been echoed by Gerald's story.

Emanuel, or 'Manny', as he was affectionately known by the many, many champion fighters he nurtured, remains among the most decorated and most esteemed coaches in boxing history. He was a self-taught 'natural' who had won a list of amateur titles before inexplicably quitting boxing in his early twenties. He had stopped fighting to take up the more stable trade of electrician in order to support his family. He had stumbled into coaching somewhat by chance when his younger brother pestered him into teaching him to box. He promptly taught that kid brother all the way to a Golden Gloves title. On the back of that success, he was asked to teach a few of the kid's club mates, too. Soon, another of his pupils won the title, and then another and then another and then another. Before long, word had spread around the country of this young coach in Detroit who somehow turned every kid he touched into a national champion. Now, the pros and the big names wanted to see if that magic could work on them too. It could. Though still in his late twenties, Emanuel was on his way to a glorious career running corners.

Somewhat like the afore mentioned Cus D'Amato, Emanuel took a philosophical view of pugilism, viewing boxing as an art form that transcended its violent aspects.

'When I was a little kid I wanted to be an artist or painter,' Manny once revealed, 'but once I got into boxing, all I wanted to do was to box...I just love the rhythm of seeing a man dance, slip punches...I would see them and be mesmerised.'

In 1980, Steward guided Texan fighter Hilmer Kenty to the world lightweight title. This would be the first of an incredible *forty-one* world champions that Steward would train over his glittering career. This list would eventually include household names such as Lennox Lewis and Wladimir Klitschko. By the mid 1980's, Steward's Kronk Gym had become a renowned boxing fortress and a worldwide brand name.

'There's not as much oxygen in that hot gym and I think it's great for conditioning,' Emanuel once said when asked about his unusual technique of keeping the temperature of his gym at a roasting 95 degrees. 'If there is one abiding theme in the gym, it's the withering work in the ring. Those not fit do not survive.'

The most famous and arguably most successful of Manny's protégés would be Tommy 'Hit Man' Hearns. The legendry Hit Man credited Steward with helping him evolve from a mediocre contender into a multi-weight world champion and one of the most feared fighters of his generation. More than that, and perhaps more significantly for our purposes, Hearns also praised Steward as being a paternal force of positive guidance, both in and out of the ring:

'I had Emanuel Steward in my life to help guide me, to help me become the man that I am today,' Tommy said, 'he instilled so much in my life. He wasn't just a trainer to me; he was like a dad to me. He started teaching me things, and I saw my life change.'

Tommy, who incidentally had been the fighter Gerald most idolised growing up, the boxer whose style he most closely tried to emulate, clearly knew his career had been in safe hands with Emanuel. The Steward stable clearly strived to provide a protective and progressive system for its young fighters. By the time Gerald McClellan came through the doors of the Kronk Gym, he was a fledgling pro with amateur championship pedigree. He was a ferocious fireball of endless potential. He was also a restless, troubled kid full of pent-up rage and with a penchant for making bad decisions. It seemed that a paternal figure with a protective and progressive system was exactly what he needed.

'Our father was very abusive when we were growing up,' Lisa confided in me. 'Never towards us, but towards our mother. Gerald had a lot of issues from that and he had a lot of anger towards our dad because of it.'

This latest revelation, one of alleged frequent domestic violence in the McClellan household, echoed aspects of an interview of Manny's I had studied previously. In it, Manny had stated of Gerald, 'When he started at the Kronk he was very much a Tommy Hearns clone, trying to box and move like Tommy, but definitely needed some tweaking. Tommy had been his hero. Unfortunately for Gerald, I had Tommy. I had Michael Moorer, Michael Bennt, I had Oba Carr, Leonzer Barber and all those guys...I spent most of my time working with Tommy and Michael Moorer. Gerald started taking guys out and he had demons inside him from his father. So, when he started taking guys out he fell in love with this power he never realised he had, because it was like a release...Every time he got in the ring he saw his father.'

I needed to know if this was true; did Gerald really envision his father's face all the times he was blasting guys unconscious? I asked Lisa the question.

'I would definitely agree with Emanuel there,' Lisa confirmed to me without hesitation. 'Gerald probably did picture our dad when he got in the ring. Our dad could be a very disrespectful person and now that he was grown, Gerald wouldn't let him dominate him. He had a lot of anger and hatred for how he treated our mother.'

I felt a pang of sympathy for Gerald. I thought about my own parents' car crash of a marriage and how growing up in a household of such tension had at times marred my own youth. I could relate to his seeking some form of cathartic release for his anger and frustration (in my case, that's probably why I first picked up a pen).

Had Gerald's explosive releases of stress been confined to the controlled setting of the boxing arena, then his inner demons may have proved manageable, if not altogether healthy. The problem was that Gerald was also lashing out at the world beyond the doors of the gym. There was an arrest after Gerald chased down and beat up a motorist who had accidently scraped his parked car. On another occasion, he allegedly flashed a stainless-steel revolver at police officers during a traffic stop. Both of these charges were in fact still pending at the time of the Benn fight.

Gerald had actually suffered the first defeat of his career whilst wearing Kronk colours. Significantly, he had prepared for this fight without Emanuel's tutelage, as Steward was preoccupied with readying Tommy Hearns for his second super-fight against Sugar Ray Leonard. Just as significantly, Steward had left Gerald to train under the care of a young underling - a novice coach in a pilot's cap, an eager-to-please upstart named Stan Johnson.

Going into his bout with veteran Dennis Milton in June 1989, Gerald had been unbeaten with ten straight wins all by knock out. New Yorker Milton was a vastly more experienced pro however, and became the first to seriously frustrate the G-Man on his way to winning a six round decision. Speaking to me from his home in the Bronx, the gentlemanly Milton kindly gave me a brief overview of the encounter:

'Gerald was the most dangerous in boxing at that time. I out-boxed and out-smarted him when I was right. I went back to the ropes and didn't let him touch me with that left hook to the body. I had the experience to let him come forwards and make him miss.'

Touchingly, Dennis finished our conversation by asking me to send his warmest regards to Gerald and Lisa. Ironically, he also pointed out that he is now heavily involved with the charity Ring10, an organisation which is dedicated to helping fighters after retirement: 'In boxing we got a brotherhood, as you know, Wayne. Boxing hasn't always done enough to look after its own. Now we just try to give something back to our own.'

That first defeat had a bad effect on Gerald. Dejected and lacking concentration, he went on to lose his next fight just three months later – an eight round decision against Ralph Ward. These two defeats would be the only losses blotting Gerald's record by the time he fought Benn six years later. When he rediscovered his focus, the G-Man went on an incredible six year run that saw him destroy opponent after opponent. When Emanuel was asked about those two unexpected defeats, he was more than willing to shoulder at least some of the blame.

'In hindsight,' Manny explained, 'Gerald was a twenty-one year old kid with no rounds under his belt going in with an experienced and slick pro (Milton), who had beaten everyone as an amateur. So, it was wrong and the guy I had looking after him, Stan Johnson, was wrong for him because he was a "yes man".'

'We started afresh in 1990 and I became quite personal with Gerald,' Manny went on. 'Gerald was a lost soul after everybody wrote him off after his losses. He also needed a bit of a father figure. He stayed with me and it's true I tooted him as the best of the lot. But in hindsight, that was wrong because he didn't have the mentality.'

When I asked Lisa about Gerald moving into Steward's family home in Detroit, she replied fondly, 'Emanuel loved Gerald and he was good for him. Gerald loved him too, but he would also get homesick. He would come back home to Freeport whenever he could; he loved to be at home. I remember, he would only be supposed to come back here for the weekend. But on Monday morning he would still be here and Manny would be banging on our front door to drag him back to the gym.'

Lisa was chuckling when she said this. I found myself smiling at the image of Steward at the door and the G-Man upstairs, peeping sheepishly from beneath his bed-sheets. It was a show of pure devotion on Manny's part; the father figure enforcing necessary discipline for the greater good of his talented yet wayward apprentice. Again, the parallels with Cus and Tyson are obvious – whenever mad Mike decided to go AWOL, old authoritarian Cus would send his men out to the mean streets of Brooklyn to drag the rebellious teenage Tyson back to his boxing Utopia of the Catskill Mountains. Like Mike, it seemed apparent that Gerald had an angel on one shoulder and a chip on the other.

Learning the nuances of that deep and sincere bond between Gerald and Manny adds yet another layer of emotion to the story. I watch back the tape of Gerald knocking out Julian Jackson to claim the WBC world middleweight title and then jumping into the arms of the smiling Manny. This was their dream and they had done it. I replayed the post-fight interview; Gerald with his new green and gold belt fastened around his waist, brimming with self-pride and adulation, Manny grinning at his boy's shoulder, telling the cameras he knew this one would never go the distance; Gerald, pumped with adrenaline, saying matter-of-factly, 'He would have had to kill me to beat me.'

At ringside for that first Jackson fight, Carl King, the son and heir of Don, had spent the duration of the contest volubly cheering on Jackson – he was their boy going into that fight and Gerald wasn't. Now that Gerald had annihilated the old hitter, Carl and Don were quickly in the ring to pose for pictures with the new young champion – this was the King's tried and tested method. Sandwiched there between Manny and Don in that instant, with his right arm held aloft and his future surely lined with gold, Gerald appears more like a man with an angel on one shoulder and the devil of the other.

The temptations of the devil are hard to resist, as many great men have found to their demise. All too soon after that night of glory, McClellan and Steward would be on frosty terms, the inept Stan Johnson would be in Gerald's corner, and Don the devil's slimy smile would be hiding the knowledge that Gerald was sticking it to his girlfriend.

'We always had disagreements,' Emanuel said later of his rift with Gerald. 'He was always wanting to work on footwork based on closing in and not even finding openings, but making openings. Everything else was a chore for him so we never got on boxing-wise and training-wise. But he had almost unlimited potential physically...He was one of the best jab artists I've seen, let alone worked with...We split because he had been convinced that he could survive without a manager...He was virtually on his own over there, making his own decisions. If I had been with Gerald McClellan, I don't think the tragedy would have happened.'

When Emanuel Steward passed away from colon cancer in 2012, the sport of boxing rightly mourned his passing. Tommy Hearns wept publically. Great fighters and sports writers from across the globe attended a ceremony in his honour. Gerald McClellan was not among them.

'I couldn't bring myself to tell Gerald that Emanuel passed,' Lisa explained. 'With his short-term memory being what it is, I knew he would be very upset, but then he would forget after a while. So then I would eventually have to explain it again and we would have to go through him being upset all over again. It was too much to face at that point.'

The burden of having to make such decisions is unimaginable. Eventually though, Lisa did take the step of informing Gerald that his great mentor had passed away.

'He was very upset,' Lisa said. 'He has retained the information. He knows that Emanuel has passed away. He still mentions him often. He'll never forget Emanuel.'

Emanuel never forgot Gerald either. In another display of genuine affection, Manny left Gerald a little something in his will. Clearly, any ill-feeling from their fallout in the 90's had not lingered.

Gerald and Emanuel had been a formidable partnership. Now, one half of that partnership is dead and the other is in no fit state to wax lyrical. Neither party ever publically clarified the exact details of their rift, but Lisa's assessment seems a fair one; now that he was champ, Gerald didn't need another daddy figure telling him what to do. He had Stan and Donnie to follow him around and obey his commands. He had Don King setting up the big fights and he had Don King's woman in his bed. If Manny wanted to occupy himself with other champions like Michael Moorer and Thomas Hearns, then he could just go ahead.

Like Tyson at the end of '89, Gerald McClellan had felt certain that he was master of his own destiny.

9

A Rude Awakening

'But whoever lives by the truth comes into the light.' John 3:21.

June 1995 - Gerald was still unconscious, still lost in the ominous depths of a coma, still lying prone in a Milwaukee hospital, still booked in under a fake name so that Don King couldn't find him. For his family, this hospital had become a second home. The staff and the relatives of other patients had become temporary friends and confidants.

'The relatives of the other patients became like family members for a time,' Lisa told me. 'They would talk to us about their family member's situation and we would talk to them about Gerald's situation, and sometimes we'd cry on each other. It helped because we were all going through the same thing and experiencing the same fears. Our family members would take it in turns to be at the hospital in the week around work and such. At the weekends, we would all be there. Everyone would be there.'

I was absorbing every word again, letting Lisa's voice transport me to that hospital room in 1995. In my mind I could almost reach out and touch Gerald's hand.

'There were two other guys in the same big room as Gerald,' Lisa continued. 'One was a black guy who had been in a car accident. The other was a white guy who had been hit over the head with something. They had both suffered brain injuries, and at first they were both semi-conscious and blind.'

Every sentence had me more tightly gripped. Lisa continued at her own pace.

'The doctors had warned us that if Gerald regained consciousness, there was a chance that he might also be blind. They were testing his eyes with a light every day and he wasn't "tracking". They call it tracking when your eyes follow something, you know? Like even if you don't mean to follow something with your eyes, your brain makes you do it automatically. So, they said Gerald's eyes were not tracking at all.'

I could only imagine the family's anguish.

'But we had hope, because the two other guys in the room who were both blind, at some point they could both suddenly see again. It was crazy, but one day they would be lying in the bed unable to see, then the next day we would walk in and one of them would be walking around talking to people. With a brain injury, sometimes it can just be the swelling around the optical nerve that affects the sight. When the swelling goes down, the vision can sometimes come back. So, we had hope that Gerald would see.'

Sometimes, it's the hope that kills you, I thought. I asked gently about the moment that Gerald had finally regained consciousness. Lisa's voice pitched.

'Every day,' she began, 'we would all be around the bed, just talking among ourselves and waiting. Every day, our dad would beat Gerald on his chest and shout at him. He would beat on his chest and say, "Wake up, man! This is your Dad! I know you're in there, boy. Wake up, man!" He would say that over and over and beat him on his chest.'

The image made my heart beat fast.

'Then one day out of nowhere,' Lisa pushed on, 'my dad was beating him on the chest like that and Gerald just said "Damn, you don't have to hit me in my chest that fucking hard!"'

This was unbelievable. My own heart was racing as I listened.

'That's what he said,' Lisa's tone lilted at the memory and she repeated Gerald's words again, 'You don't have to hit me in my chest that fucking hard!'

I had tears in my eyes now and I'm not ashamed to say it. The phone was pressed against my ear. The sudden sense of relief in that hospital room must have been overwhelming.

'We all just stopped talking and looked at each other,' Lisa carried on. 'It was like, wah? Gerald just spoke?! Did he just speak?! We couldn't believe it. We all just started hugging each other and called the nurse.'

I felt like hugging someone now just from hearing the story. I'm a sensitive soul I know, but if that didn't move you I'd go get your pulse checked.

Just like that, as suddenly as he had slipped under, Gerald McClellan had re-emerged to the land of the living – or at least a part of him had. The family's ordeal was not over yet, of course. This was a start. It was progress. He had swum upwards out of the darkness towards something resembling light. Weeks of anguished prayers and medical care had restored their son and brother to consciousness. It would be a daily strain now to discover exactly how much of him had been saved.

10

Daddy's Boy

'It is easier to build strong children than to repair broken men.' Fredrick Douglas, Writer and Social Reformer.

One night whilst working on the book, I found myself pouring my heart out to Lisa about the agony of missing my daughter. Due to a 'breakdown in communication' with my child's mother, I have not seen my daughter in almost a year. The pain is constant and unbearable and I try my best to swallow it and keep going. I miss my baby. Now, with both her birthday and Christmas fast approaching, my insides were a dam of emotion ready to burst open again.

I later apologised to Lisa for my digression, but she surprised me again by encouraging me to talk about it. I took comfort in her words and it helped me to open up to someone I have such respect for. Lisa assured me that my little girl will still think of me often (my greatest fear is that she doesn't), and that there will be a time in the future when she comes to find me (my greatest hope is that she will). It was a blessing to become more acquainted with Lisa's softer side.

In talking about my painful situation, I had also inadvertently opened the door to a candid discussion on Lisa and Gerald's relationship with their father. I asked Lisa directly if she still loves her dad.

'Hell no, I don't!' she replied instantly. 'But I ain't no little girl either. I ain't going by what someone brainwashed me. My feelings are what I seen for myself.'

'I know you have had problems,' I reasoned, 'but is there really nothing left for him?'

'No,' Lisa said decisively. 'I gave up in October when he was here last and I told him he would never see Gerald again either. He was going to hit me because he had got drunk and was mad at Todd and he took it out on me. So I stood toe-to-toe with him and told him I wasn't my mom and I wasn't scared of him. He call me a bitch and I told him he had to leave and he was NEVER welcome to come back.'

Wow! – Families, eh? Who'd have 'em?

I digested this revelation and told Lisa that her family sounded a bit like mine; God knows, we have had more than our share of feuding down the years.

'Honey,' Lisa replied, 'You don't know the half of it.'

The thing is, I actually did know the half of it – or at least, I had studied and researched enough news archives on the McClellans to have developed some understanding of the friction. I was informed enough to realise that that this unfortunate recent incident was a flare up of a deep-rooted conflict.

However openly and fervently Lisa expresses her animosity towards her dad, whatever wedge had developed between Gerald and his 'pops' by the premature end of his career, Emmit McClellan had been a present figure throughout the McClellan siblings lives. He had also been the one who first encouraged the boys to take up boxing. Todd and Emmit Jr, Gerald's brothers, were apparently proficient at the sport. Gerald, of course, excelled at it.

Emmit, who earned his living as a car mechanic, had worked on his son until he performed like a well-oiled Jag. With his dad as his first trainer, Gerald had won three consecutive national Golden Gloves titles. He scored major amateur victories over fellow prospects Tim Littles, Frank Liles, Michael Moorer and Roy Jones Junior, among others. If there was tension between father and son in the early days, it certainly didn't appear to have a negative effect on Gerald's fighting ability.

Serious cracks seemed to have appeared later. Certainly, Emmit refutes Lisa's claim that her brother was haunted by childhood memories of the overbearing father and the longsuffering mother he could not protect. According to Emmit, the relationship's decline ran concurrently to the ascent of his son's success.

'Once upon a time, we were people in the ghetto,' Emmit said in a 1996 interview. 'Then he's at the top of the world. For many a day he felt he didn't need Dad anymore.'

By the time Gerald flew to London to fight Nigel Benn, it seemed he had alienated the two father figures in his life; he and Emmit were no longer on speaking terms, and Manny Steward was legally pursuing monies owed for his services rendered. Both Emmit and Emanuel would of course soften somewhat when Gerald flew home on a stretcher.

One might think that Gerald's un-promised revival from that coma would usher in a new era of peace among those around him; blessing of blessings, their boy was alive again. He was damaged and severely altered from the man he had been, but he was still with them. However, far from providing an opportunity to build bridges and write off old grudges, Gerald's slow recovery marked the advent of fresh conflict on many fronts. From my own humble but studied viewpoint, the three key factors of this feuding seem to have been love, money and justice.

By the August of 1995, Gerald was deemed well enough to leave the hospital. Soon thereafter, the McClellan family became locked in a bitter internal battle over custody of the twenty-seven year old former champion. It is almost unfathomable to consider how much had changed in the space of six months.

Now that Gerald was back in Freeport, completely blind and unable to care for himself, there was discontent over who could best provide for his many needs. Essentially, it became a tug-of-love struggle between Emmit McClellan and his three daughters. Gerald's mother, Genola, had developed a drink problem and was apparently in no fit state to be his primary caregiver. Gerald's father wanted his son to live with him. Gerald's sisters, Lisa, Sandra and Stacy, along with their closest aunt, Linda Shorter, were determined that was not going to happen.

Things came to a head when the McClellan girls claimed that Emmit had been irresponsible when left in charge of Gerald. They claimed he had twice left Gerald alone whilst supposedly watching over the disabled convalescent. On one occasion, it was claimed that Gerald had managed to end up outside in his wheelchair, rambling nonsensically at the world whilst covered in his own faeces – there could hardly have been a more degrading fall from grace for the champ.

In his own defence, Emmit claimed that this incident had been a set up arranged by his scheming daughters. He insisted that he had briefly left Gerald in the care of a female friend whilst he went to run some errands. He argued that the sisters had devised a cunning plan to make the woman leave the house, and then made it look as though Gerald had been abandoned.

These shocking allegations were among the most unsavoury morsels of testimony served up by either side at the custody hearing. Having thrown mud like that in each others' directions, it is not hard to see why there is little love lost now. But still, there was more. Custody was not the sole cause of the conflict. As ever, that man Don King was not too far removed from the unrest.

It was during the custody battle that Emmit first voiced the suggestion of foul play on Don King's part – namely, that he had stolen back Gerald's contract for the Benn fight in order to run a 'phony' one in its place. This came out as a judge attempted to make sense of Gerald's financial situation and deduce whether King, as Gerald's former promoter, retained any legal obligation to financially assist the family. On this score, the McClellan sisters seemed willing to agree with their dad. Both parties were adamant that King still had significant dues to pay their way.

Soon, both sides of the argument would be firing off conspiracy theories of fraud and deception which were pungent enough to flare the nostrils of the FBI – suddenly, this relatively minor (in world terms) family dispute might present the Federal Bureau of Investigation with a rare opportunity of finally snagging their old elusive enemy, Don King.

As the fallout progressed, the allegations grew deeper and darker than just monetary gain - much darker. Perhaps driven by their inside knowledge of Gerald's recent affair with the enigmatic Maria, both Emmit and Lisa even began hinting that Gerald's sudden demise that night in London had been premeditated; the emerging theory was that Don King had held no intention of seeing Gerald win.

'Wrong stuff went down in London,' Emmit declared at the time. 'You're dealing with the underworld here, and somebody called that number. It was far from being an accident.'

Lisa, meanwhile, threw an even bigger grenade into the warzone. She claimed to have secretly recorded a conversation with Gerald's corner-men in which they told her something potentially explosive – during the Benn fight, Gerald had complained that his mouthpiece tasted funny! Was this the reason it wouldn't stay in his mouth? Was this the reason he had suddenly sunk to his knees and then dropped into oblivion? Was this reason for all of this?

Did this tape represent a near-homicidal sabotage by an affronted organised criminal, or was it more a product of a sister's aggressive paranoia, brought on by grief? Either way, the FBI were interested enough to take possession of the recording. Naturally, I was eager to sit Lisa down to discuss this episode with me (more on that later).

The next twist in the tale came when Emmit suddenly recanted his accusations of wrong doing against Don King. This provoked fresh assertions from his daughters that Emmit had accepted hush-money from the promoter. From somewhere, a figure of $10,000 was touted as the amount Emmit had taken to close his mouth. The claims were unsubstantiated. Emmit, of course, denied it. As did the man himself, Don King.

King, in his own long-winded and narcissistic style, branded the whole sorry mess as a government backed plan to finally end his reign.

'Lisa is a very limited person,' Don raged, 'And I don't want to cast aspersions, but she's overshot the runway. She's a pawn, being used. When she brought up the FBI, this agent Warren Flagg has become obsessed with me...This culprit here is an insidious conspiracy, and she has brought it to the front, implemented by the government, a dead-set conspiracy to destroy Don King, galvanised by HBO. You can see the conspiracy out there plain as day. She done named all my enemies.'

Complicating this tangled mesh of a situation even further, the McClellan sisters had drawn swords on yet another enemy. Angie Brown, the live-in girlfriend of Gerald and mother of his young daughter, Forrest, was no longer welcome at the family home. She too had reportedly received a cheque signed by Don King. In her eyes, this was apparently an award to help her with childcare costs now that Gerald was unable to earn an income. In Lisa's eyes, it was an incentive for Angie to testify in Emmit's favour at the custody hearing.

Soon, Angie would move out of the family home and retreat to Detroit with her daughter. When I asked Lisa for details of this falling out, her reply was classic 'Lisa.'

'Nothing to tell,' she said. 'I kicked her ass every time I saw her for what she did to Gerald after he got hurt...She has an order against me contacting her for thirteen years.'

Naturally, I pushed for more information on this latest bombshell, but for once Lisa wasn't instantly forthcoming.

'If you contact her, I'll be done with you, Wayne,' was Lisa's initial response. I decided to leave that stone at least partially unturned, for the time being at least.

At the end of the turbulent custody battle, the judge sifted through the confusion of claims and counter-claims and decided on awarding guardianship to Gerald's aunt, Linda Shorter. The three sisters had won this one. The reward for their small victory was eight hours a day each of hands-on, one-to-one care for their brother. They had agreed to take it in shifts, rotating every eight hours. In time, only one of them would truly keep to this promise. In defeat, Emmit couldn't hide his bitterness. He also hinted that Gerald's best interests were never his daughters' primary goal.

'My daughter loused things up,' he said of Lisa. 'I raised Gerald to be successful and they barred me away, changing the phone to where I can't even call...I got railroaded and kicked out...My daughters were there for the money, and not a lot of money. But we're talking about people who never had more than a couple thousand...I'm done with the family for the rest of my life.'

Lisa hit back, saying of her father at the time, 'If he dies, don't even call me about the funeral.'

God, Gerald; that was some defeat.

11

Donald King Versus The FBI

'You catch more flies with honey than with vinegar.' English proverb.

FBI agent Warren Flagg was once described by *Sports Illustrated* as the Captain Ahab to Don King's Moby Dick. The idea was that veteran Warren had long been driven by a monomaniacal obsession with finally reeling in the flamboyant one and ending his perceived reign of terror. That being the case, Agent Flagg must have thought he had finally got a bite when he received a call from the writer and documentary maker, Jack Newfield. Jack shared Agent Flagg's fascination with Don King's shady activities and had spent much of his illustrious career writing about the man. Now, in early 1995, these two men were about to share a conversation regarding a young woman in Illinois; a woman who claimed to have hard evidence implicating their arch nemesis.

During another fascinating transatlantic phone call in 2017, Lisa McClellan would kindly relay all the gory details to me. As always, my ears were wide open and ready to devour every single word she said to me.

'This was still in 1995, Wayne,' Lisa began. 'Gerald was still in the hospital, still under the fake name so that nobody knew where he was. At this time, I was still going to nursing school and I had found that I was struggling to keep up with the psychology lectures. So, I had bought myself a small tape recorder so that I could listen back to the lectures at home.'

'One day, I got a call from Stan Johnson and Donnie Pendleton. They said, "You need to come to Milwaukee. We need to talk to you quick." So, I got in the car and I drove two hours to Milwaukee. I didn't know what they were going to say, but I had my tape recorder in the car. I decided I would keep it in my pocket and use it to record the conversation. I met them in the bar of a hotel and as soon as I walked in, I clicked on the tape.'

'Stan and Donnie told me that, "Don told us to get the fuck out of England and keep our fucking mouths shut. Don knew that Gerald was fucking Maria Russey and they had argued about it and Gerald had told Don to suck his dick...They put something on Gerald's mouthpiece." That's what they said.'

This was more dynamite stuff – an accusation of foul play. I let Lisa keep flowing at her own pace.

'They kept talking and I heard my tape click off in my pocket,' she continued. 'These two guys were so fucking stupid that I told them I needed to get something from the car and went out and changed the tape and came back in to record the rest of the conversation. They told me that something had been done to Gerald's mouthpiece.'

No more beating about the bush, I needed to know once and for all what Lisa really believes happened that night in London - I asked Lisa outright now whether she truly believes what happened to Gerald was a tragic accident or an act of deliberate, criminal sabotage.

'Do you believe, in your heart of hearts, that his mouthpiece was poisoned?'

'Yes,' Lisa confirmed, 'I can't prove it, but I believe it.'

'So it was a mafia hit?' I asked without ambiguity. This was some allegation and I needed perfect clarity. There could be no room at all for misunderstanding.

'Basically,' Lisa said. 'We can't prove it, but that's what I believe.'

My mind was blown again. It all sounded so outlandish, yet so possible. Did a world of fight fans really bear witness to a cunning assassination attempt without knowing it? Was one of the most thrilling fights in boxing history really a cover for a powerful man's cruel act of vengeance? It was perplexing to consider.

'After the fight,' Lisa continued, 'I had been called by Jack Newfield. Jack Newfield put me in touch with Warren Flagg, the FBI agent who has spent his career chasing up Don King. Jack and Warren Flag began speaking to me on the phone almost every night. I made a copy of the tapes and sent them to Jack and he sent them to Warren.'

This was becoming more and more like the plot from a Pacino movie. The FBI now had possession of two tapes in which two men audibly implicated Don King in an alleged criminal act – a full-blown felony which had robbed a young fighter of his career, his health and most of his life. Surely, this was their chance to finally nail him.

'So, why is Don still a free man?' I asked the obvious question.

'The problem was that the tape was obviously not recorded with Stan and Donnie's consent,' Lisa explained. 'In the United States, it can't be used as evidence in a court of law if it's recorded without consent. The FBI pulled Stan and Donnie in for a deposition, but they denied it. They denied ever saying it.'

'They were scared?' I thought out loud.

'Absolutely they were scared,' Lisa agreed as though it made perfect sense for them to be terrified.

'Were you not scared?' I asked.

'I was never scared for a second,' Lisa replied defiantly. 'For a start, Don would have had to be the most fucking stupid person on the planet to have anything done to me whilst it was all in the spotlight. I even called Don's office and I told him, "I'm not afraid of you. I'm going to protect my brother if that means going toe-to-toe with you."'

With Lisa, none of this ever sounds like 'big talk.' She delivers every sentence with such conviction, such fire in her voice.

'But one thing did happen that I believe was Don trying to intimidate me,' Lisa carried on. 'One night, I was home alone with my daughter and a car pulled up in the driveway. A guy just sat there, parked in my driveway. I know this was coming from Don, trying to scare me. I wasn't scared at all. I went outside and tapped on this guy's window and asked him, "What the fuck you doing?" The guy just looked at me and drove off. I had written down the number of his plates. But when the FBI ran the plates it came back as stolen. The car wasn't stolen, but the tags were stolen. I couldn't prove it was from Don, but I know it was.'

I asked Lisa if she was not worried at all about making these revelations to me now – was she not concerned that when these bold exposures became public record in my book, there might be repercussions. After all, she is not a feisty twenty-six year old woman anymore. She is a feisty forty-eight year old grandmother.

'I'm not scared,' she said. 'If I called Don King's office today and said it's Lisa McClellan, they would act all nice and say, "Hey, how's Gerald doing? Send him our love."

But we never asked for anything from Don King other than what was owed to Gerald. That's all we wanted.'

'But Wayne,' she added pertinently, 'you do need to highlight this: the mouthpiece story came from the same two guys who made up the dog stories about Gerald, and 95% of that was bullshit. Stan is such a fucking liar that you don't know what to believe. Like when he said Gerald punched out his front teeth in the gym. That's a fucking lie! He lost his teeth 'cos he's a fucking drug addict.'

I was on the edge of my seat again. Every sentence seemed to carry another heat-seeking missile. Pinpointing the truth in this increasingly tangled mess became even more impossible when she revealed that Stan and Donnie had soon started taking aim at each other.

'Donnie said later that Don had paid Stan $10,000 to put something on the mouthpiece,' Lisa dropped yet another bombshell. 'After the fight, Don gave Donnie $3,000 and told him to get out of England. But he gave Stan $10,000. They both just wanted to get paid and get out of there. But they both lie so much, Wayne, we just don't know what to believe and we have no proof.'

My mind was swimming with intrigue again, overdosing on elaborations that just might be as true as they are sensational.

'I called Don King one day and he told me –'Lisa broke off, trying to recall the exact words Don had said to her. She struggled to remember them exactly. 'It was some kind of saying about getting more with honey than vinegar.'

I knew the saying she was phishing for. I understood the implications of it and so did she.

'I can't remember the exact saying, Wayne,' Lisa said. 'But he was basically telling me I would be better off keeping my mouth shut.'

Clearly, Lisa had no intention of reaching for that honey jar anytime soon, God bless her. By the time this latest phone call ended and I settled back to read over my notes, I couldn't help feeling that my book might soon be throwing rocks at a bee-hive.

12

This Ain't No Kronk!

'The point is to not confuse objectivity with truth.' Jack Newfield, Muckraking Journalist.

So, Gerald McClellan had survived. After months on the edge of the abyss, a depleted version of the G-Man had clawed its way back from the precipice and was going home to the family. For a man in desperate need of calm and recuperation, the setting he was returning to was anything but ideal.

That long, terrifying stay in hospital had devastated his nearest and dearest. By late 1995, the McClellans had reached the brink of emotional and financial exhaustion. The dispute with Don King was just heating up. The internal feuding between the sisters and their father over Gerald's care was bubbling over. Gerald's mother was drinking herself senseless to cope with the stress. His brother Todd was heading to prison on an unrelated battery charge. The family was besieged by problems and to top it all off, the city of Freeport had been buried beneath a sudden pile of snow.

'I remember there was a terrible blizzard that November,' Lisa tells me. It's funny what people remember when recalling the most testing episodes of their lives.

But snow certainly wasn't the only thing getting under Lisa's feet. She had decided that Gerald's girlfriend, Angie Brown, was now an enemy and had taken to 'kicking her ass' whenever they crossed paths around Freeport. Angie would soon pack her bags and vanish to Detroit, taking Gerald's daughter with her.

Although Lisa had warned me off contacting Ms Brown for comment, I was eager to learn more about this falling out. Eventually, Lisa opened up to me with even more explosive revelations.

'I kicked her ass for what she did to Gerald after he got hurt,' Lisa said. 'She stole all Gerald's jewellery and clothes and gave them to other men. That's why I kicked her ass...She was sleeping around in Gerald's house after he got hurt, while he was in the hospital. She had slept with every friend, or should I say so called friend, Gerald had. Then she slept with a boyfriend of mine so I kicked her ass again.'

'Sounds like the kind of girl I should be looking up,' I joked. Lisa took it as such.

'Word on the street is Angie got a hella mouthpiece on her,' she added, 'if you know what I mean.'

I know what you mean, Lisa. I thought of Gerald's passionate affair with Maria; maybe what's good for the goose is good for the gander. I wasn't sure if they have that saying in Illinois.

'I let her live with me for a while and she had a lot of traffic in her bedroom,' Lisa continued. 'Gerald wasn't perfect, but she knew what he had been doing.'

I asked Lisa about the money that Angie Brown had reportedly received from Don King - thousands of dollars apparently given to assist her with childcare costs now that Gerald could no longer provide for his daughter. Yet again, Lisa's response was completely unexpected.

'Don gave Angie money because he was fucking her,' Lisa threw this latest revelation at me like a rock. I was stunned. 'Don was fucking her while she was in London to visit Gerald in the hospital. He did it to get back at Gerald for the Maria Russey affair.'

I was beginning to see Freeport as an American version of my hometown of Batley; a lot of people are having sex with a lot of people they shouldn't be having sex with. Lust makes the world go round. Still, this was another fascinating development – that old rogue Don King really hadn't taken it lying down, so to speak. Men like Don can ill-afford to be humiliated.

I asked Lisa where all of this had left Gerald's relationship with his daughter, Forrest. How did she feel about all this tension? How had she been affected by her mother taking out an injunction against her aunt? Does she visit her father these days?

'She calls,' Lisa replied simply. 'She has been away at school the last five years...We're OK.'

As a writer, this story had become everything I could have wished for and more. My every conversation with Lisa seemed to present another storm of controversy to dance in. I let each one rain over me and I could never pretend not to be experiencing some electrifying thrill at each new thunder bolt of sensationalism that struck me. I felt certain that all of these separate but entangled conflicts and un-conjugals would make for entertaining reading; people are fascinated by the folly of other people; we crave drama - that's what the lucrative twin industries of literature and film are made of. At the same time though, I couldn't shake off the unbearable sadness of it all. This was not a soap opera where fictional characters disappear into thin air with the ending of each episode. These were real people making real mistakes and inflicting very real pain upon each other.

And sitting there at the centre of it all was a blind man oblivious to what his world had become.

Heartbreakingly, Gerald had initially refused to accept or acknowledge that he was blind. He came home to Freeport with no memory of what had happened in the Benn fight and little understanding of why his life was suddenly so different. Desperate for some shred of self-preservation, he would tell himself and his sisters a thin cover story that he couldn't see anything because it was particularly dark today. Depending on the situation, Lisa would sometimes indulge this excuse to prevent him from getting upset.

'Sometimes, I'd tell him I can't see too well either because it's very dark in here today,' Lisa told me.

Other situations were harder to find excuses for. Ignoring his own inability to see, Gerald would occasionally ask to watch a tape of the Benn fight. On other occasions, he would demand to know why he wasn't getting ready for another fight. Sometimes, he would proudly ask visitors to the family home if they wanted tickets to come see him fight in the future. Hearing her brother say such things with no concept of their absurdity must have cut Lisa through the middle.

Blindness was not the only issue the family had to adapt to. Gerald had come out of hospital dangerously underweight at 128lbs . Several months of been fed by intravenous drip had stripped him to the bone. But within weeks of returning home to his sisters' loving care, his weight had ballooned to an all time high. Lisa's home cooked feasts had piled on the pounds, and with Gerald under no strict training regime for the first time in his life, there was little to burn off the calories.

In a bid to bring his weight back under control, the sisters devised a clever ploy. They would coax Gerald onto a treadmill in the kitchen by telling him he was back in the Kronk gym and he was back in training. Sometimes, Gerald would go along with it. He would walk as best he could on the conveyor belt with his sisters helping his balance. But on other occasions, he would suddenly be struck by a realisation that he wasn't back in that sacred old gym in Detroit – perhaps some mental flashback to the gym's stifling temperature of 95 degrees, maybe an unbidden memory of the scent of leather and perspiration, the thump and rattle of heavy-bags getting drilled, or the sound of Emanuel and other coaches barking out instructions. These were all absent. Discovering the lie would devastate him. 'This ain't no Kronk!' Gerald would suddenly scream at his sisters, tears filling his eyes. They would be forced to end the training session there and lead him back to the quiet of his armchair. Hurt and confused, he would cry to himself until the memory left him.

Adding to the mounting stress, it was now difficult for the sisters to communicate with Gerald on even a basic level. Anything they said to him had to be yelled at high volume and repeated several times before he made any sense of it. Though it was initially believed he was now 70% deaf, Gerald's hearing has in fact been largely unaffected by his brain injury. It is his ability to comprehend what is being said that causes the problems. He hears the words, but he struggles to understand them.

'Gerald's hearing is fine,' Lisa explains. 'The problem is with comprehension. The damage to his brain was caused by it swelling against the skull. So it wasn't just a part of the brain that was affected. The whole brain was affected.'

With such damage inflicted, the struggle for Gerald to make sense of his new existence must have been overwhelming. To go from champion Alpha male to blind dependent, with no real linear understanding of how and why, must be a living nightmare. It is no surprise that he quickly developed a fear of abandonment and yearned for the comfort of physical contact to reassure him. He would demand to hold the hand of whomever he was speaking to and he would squeeze it tight. He also developed a childlike affection, relishing the touch of a hand against his cheek or on his shoulder.

As time progressed, Gerald devised his own little game in a bid to claw back some form of control. When asking questions about the present state of affairs, he would demand that his sisters give him a $20 bill from their purse for him to hold. In his mind, this would give them an incentive to tell him the truth.

'Do I still have my cars?' he would ask, referring to the growing fleet of vehicles he had collected prior to the Benn fight.

'Yes, Gerald, you still have your cars,' the sisters would assure him. They would stop short of pointing out that he could never possibly drive them again.

'Do I still have my dogs?' he would ask after his beloved pride of pitbulls. 'If I still have my dogs, then give me $20 to hold and I'll give it back to you later.'

Counting on his lack of sight, the sisters would often give Gerald a $1 bill instead. Retaining some of his old cunning, Gerald would counter this trick by threatening to rip the bill up in front of them.

'This doesn't feel like a twenty,' he would say. 'If it's a twenty, I bet you'd be mad if I tore it up.'

He would tease them by tearing a small piece of the corner, but then he would stop and tuck the note down his sock for safe keeping. If his sisters wanted the cash back badly enough, they would wait until later when he was sleeping, or when his terribly defective short term memory rubbed out all knowledge of the money's presence.

This was life now for the McClellans. For Lisa, in particular, it was only the beginning of a long and lonely journey. As the siblings strived to make the best of their new circumstances, journalists around the world were busy writing of Gerald's plight. Soon, the G-Man would be making headlines for his past life outside of boxing, and public sympathy towards him would suddenly be on the slide.

13

Dog Eat Dog World

'Despite everything that has been written about Gerald McClellan over the years, he is not the bogeyman, he is just a man.' Bernard O'Shea, The Price of War.

As a writer and passionate boxing aficionado, I am involved with several online boxing sites and forums. Some are better than others. For me, *Boxing Legion* is by far and away the best one. This page attracts a massive following from Britain, America, Australia, Africa and beyond. Many of its members are ex-fighters and current pros; the rest are a motley crew of passionate armchair experts, completely certain of their own pugilistic wisdom – God bless them. These forums offer a brilliant mixture of banter, debate and discussion on the hardest game. From the old hypothetical 'Tyson or Ali' squabble to arguments over more contemporary rivalries, like AJ Vs Wilder or Fury Vs the rest of the world, nothing gets missed.

I have long since realised that when it comes to boxing, men find it impossible not to express a strong opinion. Perhaps due to the ostensibly 'macho' nature of our beloved sport (the fact that it essentially involves men being men), it seems that when faced with a boxing related hypothesis, no man is ever willing to utter the three most emasculating of words – 'I don't know.'

Certainly, when the name 'Gerald McClellan' is brought up, there is no sitting on the fence. The forum will suddenly explode into life at the very mention of his name. Arguments will erupt. His boxing record and his ring legacy will inevitably be brushed aside, his achievements reduced to a mere footnote, as the G-Man's fans and detractors dissolve into heated debates on ethics, morality and animal cruelty. I have witnessed these arguments unfold many times and have occasionally allowed myself to be dragged into them. As a writer, I can never resist slipping in a quick plug of this book; whether they love Gerald or detest him, he surely presents a subject worthy of being read up on.

As an exercise in gauging current public perception of Gerald McClellan, and also as a genuine attempt to raise additional funds for his family, I shared a post on a few of the more prominent boxing forums. I included the link to Lisa's 'Go-Fund-Me' page and left a few lines about myself, my project and about the McClellan's ongoing financial struggles. The response was immediate and fascinating.

'Great middleweight...Terrible shame what happened to him.'

'Very exciting fighter...This guy would destroy any middleweight around today.'

'The Benn fight was brutal...Never seen a fight like it.'

'Didn't this guy torture dogs? That's not right, man.'

'No sympathy for monsters like him...Karma is a bitch!'

'How can you people compare a dog's life to a man's life? The guy is disabled! Show some respect.'

'Fuck Gerald McClellan! He saw the blood and he heard the yelps of pain and he deserves what happened to him.'

'What about his family? Don't they deserve better?'

'We supposed to care about this guy just cos he boxed for a living? Fuck him.'

'Everyone is a judge. He put his life on the line for our entertainment.'

'He killed dogs for kicks. He deserves to suffer. End of!'

Comments like the above continued to be fired from all angles and all corners of the cyber-world. Like Gerald's punches, they came thick and fast. For many, the rumours of Gerald's involvement in underground dog-fighting are enough to condemn the man to Hell and that's that. For others, his boxing career and his private lifestyle can be measured as completely separate entities. Beyond that, there are some for whom a life of blindness and disability absolves the man of his alleged wrongdoings.

Of course, I have long since been aware of the sinister tales of Gerald's alleged pastimes. As a fan of his exciting fighting style first and foremost, I had never really considered it a major issue in my looking up to him. I admired his ring craft and his self-belief and his phenomenal power and I didn't really care much about what he did or didn't do in his spare time. Perhaps I had greatly underestimated just how strongly many people felt about the horror stories of depravity surrounding him. Now, I was seeing it face on. Now, I was growing curious for details of what he had actually been involved in.

I observed with keen interest and mixed feelings as the conflicting points piled up beneath my online post. On the one hand, it bode well for me and my little book that Gerald could stir up such passion from my target audience, both positive and negative. On the other, it made me question for the first time my own unrelenting fascination with the man. I would hasten to point out that there is nothing wrong or unnatural about being intrigued by any public figure with a famed dark side to their personality. Serial killer documentaries are never short of an audience. The Kray twins will no doubt be studied and mythologized long after East London is reduced to rubble. Adolf Hitler will be written about for as long as there is ink. Athletes, singers and actors with a controversial edge – OJ Simpson, Mike Tyson, Sean Penn, Eminem, etc – surely all garner more public interest for their battles with inner-demons than do their apparently more well-balanced counterparts. It is human nature to slow down and stare at the car crash. Every fairytale needs the bad guy element.

If I am going to explore the story of Gerald McClellan, then I must explore it all. I cannot just write of his glories and of the tragedy that prevented him from adding to them. I cannot just write of his sister's tireless devotion to whatever was left of him after that fateful February night. It is important for any credible writer to tell the truth, even if that truth might bring moisture to his eyes and leave a nasty taste in the mouth.

Let's picture a scene: It's the mid 1990's, an ordinary downtown street in Illinois; the sun is shining between tenement buildings, traffic slowly snakes and beeps. We focus on a row of shops: hardware store, grocery store, pet store. At the head of an alleyway on the corner, a small tribe of young men are just hanging loose, shooting dice, killing time. There is nothing else to do. Their heads jerk around as a car pulls up to the curb. It is a freshly waxed Corvette with all the trimmings: a man's car. Around here, they would say it is the kind of car a 'baller' drives. When its doors open, the young man who steps from it does not disappoint. He is tall and lean, a trimmed moustache riding his top lip, *Bulls* vest exposing his tattooed biceps, matching baseball-cap hitched stylishly to the side. He looks like what he is: a mean son of a bitch.

The young man pauses on the sidewalk and glances towards the boys on the corner. One of them tips his chin towards him in a barely perceptible gesture of recognition. The kid feels certain he has seen the young man somewhere before, but he can't quite place him yet. The young man is a rising star, but not yet a household name. He nods back at the boy, knowing that one day kids like that will rush towards him on sight, begging for his autograph. He *knows* they will.

From the opposite end of the street, two young females are passing. Shopping bags on their arms and high-heels on their feet, their toned navels on show beneath cropped vests, they look good and they know it. They too look the young man up and down appraisingly. They make no attempt to disguise their interest. The young man holds their stares just like he holds anybody's. His eyes narrow and he licks his lips, posturing. Were he not so preoccupied, he would no doubt stop and talk to them, maybe even take the one with cornrows for a ride. But today he has no time for that. Today, he has another kind of bitch on his mind.

The young man enters the pet store and nods greetings at the decrepit old man behind the counter. The place is dingy and stinks of sawdust and animal shit. Caged birds chirp and squawk incessantly behind bars, rodents run moronically around mazes, lizards lurk behind glass. The young man bypasses all of this and bends to browse a small pen housing various dogs in separate cubicles. He scrutinises each mutt in turn, making a mental note of breed, size and sex. Finally, he selects a Labrador, the kind of dog a kid gets for Christmas and cherishes for the next twelve to fifteen years. This dog will not be resting under a tree with a bow on its collar any time soon. This dog is not so lucky.

The young man purchases the canine and carries it out to his vehicle. He places it securely in the small cage he keeps in the back. The cage is lined with newspaper to soak up any nervous piss the dog might decide to leak out. As he heads back to the driver's seat, he glances again at the boys on the corner. One of them raises a fist towards him – a sign of respect, a salute. They have figured out who he is now. He is the fighter; the fighter who keeps knocking guys out in round one. The young man tips his chin in return and climbs back in the car. He starts the ignition and sets off for home with his new toy.

When he gets home, he will take the dog down to his basement. In his basement, he has a video camera, a roll of duct tape and a caged pitbull named Deuce. In his basement there is privacy for a man to indulge his darkest desires. In his basement, there are no windows and the light cannot get through...

This is a version of Gerald McClellan which has circled and solidified itself in the two decades since the Nigel Benn encounter. For many, it is the accepted truth; they read it somewhere, so it must be true, right?

This perception of Gerald, one that sees him as the ice cold predator and woman slayer, a beast who got his kicks from watching one animal rip another one to bits on his bidding, emerged largely from stories put forwards by two men he was once close to; two men who were standing in his corner one night in London; two men who accompanied him on an ambulance ride through the lamp-lit streets of England's capital – Stan Johnson and Donnie Pendleton.

Both of these men have spoken openly to sections of the world's media about Gerald's alleged extracurricular activities. Both have sold, rather than told, stories of his rumoured bloodlust.

The horror stories of bared teeth and torn flesh were then presented to the world at large by a major publication, a 2002 book written by a well known British journalist – a book which Lisa insists to me is 'all lies.'

In typical Lisa fashion, she pulled no punches when I broached this subject: 'I never liked that black motherfucker!' she said of Donnie, taking me completely by surprise with her vernacular. I admire her unrelenting honesty. With Lisa, you always know where you stand. 'He is homeless in Milwaukee now and so deserving of it. He sold lies to the press about Gerald just to make money.'

When I asked if she could remember a certain prominent London journalist visiting her home some years back, she was just as forthcoming: 'Yes; that asshole wrote [that book]...It was all lies.'

The book she was referring to is one of the major distributors of the dog stories. I hoped in time she would give my book a less scathing review. Time will tell.

Donnie, the now homeless vagrant whom Lisa so detests, is actually a step-cousin of the McClellans. Perhaps that makes his apparent betrayal, his feeding of shock stories to the press, all the more stinging. When I look over some of the comments Donnie has made to the media over the years, it doesn't read to me as though he was outright criticising the G-Man. Rather, it comes across as a sort of misguided affection. It also reads like Donnie was just describing a world that he and 'Gerry' and Stan inhabited; the hard streets of urban Illinois, a world of brash young men and barking dogs, a do-or-die world where bad things sometimes happen and that's that.

'He was a nice, young, scary kid,' Donnie explained in one of his old paid interviews. 'He was a maniac with the pitbull dogs, man. He was like one himself; very aggressive, very crazy. He had like a yard full of pitbulls...I didn't like watching them dogs fight like that. But them dogs, they going to fight naturally anyway. Gerald always say, 'God Damn, if I gotta fight for a living, I'll be damned if them dogs ain't gotta fight for a living too. I gotta buy 'em their food. If it's a big fight and they win, they oughta be buying their own damn food.'

Stan Johnson, the pilot-cap wearing eccentric, the coach who promptly tried to fill the gigantic shoes of the great Emanuel Steward, has been just as colourful in his descriptions of Gerald over the years. In fact, some of what Stan has to say makes truly difficult reading for anyone unfamiliar with their violent subculture.

'His whole life was about fighting,' Stan declared of his ex-employer. 'He pay lotsa money on dog fights. He took money from his fights and bet [it on the dog fights]. It weren't nothing for him to go down to the projects in Chicago and bet $10,000 that his dog beat your dog. And a bunch of gang bangers with guns and drugs all came down to watch.'

'Gerald had some companionship about this one particular dog. He'd raised this dog and it had killed a few...Once this dog lost a fight and Gerald was $7,000 down. The other guy says "Hey, you wanna wash your dog off before you put him in your truck?" Gerald just pulls a nine-millimetre [pistol] out of his back pocket, aims at the dog's head, busts a cap in the dog's head and says, "Put that motherfucker in a plastic bag. I don't need 'em if they can't fight no better than that..." This is the kind of guy he was.'

Stan's stories don't end there and they don't all involve canines. He continued: 'We in Florida this one time. We in training, just before we go to fight Nigel Benn. Gerald says, "You wanna go do some shopping? So we go to the mall with the champ. We come outta the mall and in Florida they got these pretty little pelican birds, what you call 'em? Flamingos, that's it. They just walk around the mall trying to make it look pretty...But Gerald comes out and says, "Right, watch this!" And there's this flamingo walking around the road. Gerald gets close and makes a dip with the car. He speeds up the car real bad and – Boom! He hits the damn flamingo. And the flamingo flies up all over the grille and Gerald, he's laughing like it's all in Disneyland. He goes around the block and he looks at the grille and he pulls the bird feathers and he pulls the bird outta the grille...So then Gerald goes around again! The kid was a violent kid. He loved killing shit, he loved dog fights, like it was evident, he was want to go out like he went out...He was a violent, violent, violent, violent, violent person.'

The graphic tales of guts and gore from Stan don't end there: 'So he got this black Labrador, just went to the dog shop, told the man I need a dog to take care of, I'll take this Labrador home...He takes the dog down his basement and tapes the Labrador's mouth, takes his pitbull Deuce and says "Get him!" He lets Deuce start eating the dog up while he's timing it on a watch, see how long it would take his dog to kill this dog...'

Johnson claims that he asked Gerald why he felt the need to tape the dog's mouth shut - a Labrador would obviously have little chance against a pitbull even without this disadvantage. Stan claims that Gerald responded, 'Cos I just wanna see how fast my dog would kill him, for one, and for two, my dog's a championship fighter and you don't need no dog scratched up and bit by no accident. This is like sparring for my dog. This is like my dog need to taste blood every day.'

Even when Stan attempted to share a story showing Gerald's lesser known soft side, he couldn't help but spin another yarn of brutality: 'He brought Deuce down to fight this guy's dog in Chicago one time, and me an Donnie, we went down there with him...Gerald was driving his Mercedes Benz, a green car with caramel-coloured seats and he had this big, beautiful truck behind where he carried his dogs in cages. So Deuce, he winning this fight, then all of a sudden the dog got on him and started ripping Deuce's throat out...Just as his dog was getting beat, Gerald told the dude, 'Stop the fight!" And the dude said, "No man, you started the fight." And Gerald says, "You stop this motherfucking fight! I quit. Here your money"...Gerald had a nice green leather suit on. He picked his bloody dog up, threw his dog across his shoulder, blood all run down his fucking coat. Instead of putting his dog in the truck, in the cage, he put him in the backseat of the Benz, mad as hell, rubbing his dog, crying up and down the road telling, "I ain't never gonna do this shit no more, I don't know why I did this...'"

British boxing coach Martin Bowers recalled a very different side to Gerald McClellan. Martin made Gerald's acquaintance whilst the American was using the famous Peacock Gym to finish his pre-fight preparations in London.

'McClellan got a bad press around the time of the fight,' Bowers said. 'But he didn't bring any of that into the gym. He never said anything untoward about anyone. He wasn't aloof. He just did his training, had his coffee, checked his weight and talked about his dogs. He was just a genuine guy interested in his dogs and his boxing.'

For those of us unfamiliar with the underground 'sport' of dog-fighting, it presents itself as a most extreme and outlandish pastime to become entrenched in; a sort of violent 'other world' that these young men must surely seek out at the push of their own depravity. But on the streets of Chicago, the activity has been increasingly rampant since the 1980's. In fact, it is now so commonplace that many children of school age claim to have attended organised dogfights. A recent survey of 35,000 Illinoisan infants by the 'Anti-Cruelty Society' even suggested that as many as one in fifteen children have played spectator at such an event. One in seven children also said they knew such fights were taking place in their neighbourhoods.

'Dog fighting is nothing new to kids these days,' said Chicago Police Sergeant, Mark George, head of the city's Animal Crimes Unit. 'Unfortunately, it has become a part of life for many kids.'

With dog-fighting being so common and so accessible in such areas, it is easy to see how individuals, particularly the young and misguided, might be drawn into it. Familiarity does not excuse this or any crime, of course. But to young men like Gerald growing up with dog-fighting as a part of their everyday social backdrop, it must surely have felt like less of a major deal to become involved in it – a 'monkey see, monkey do' type scenario, perhaps.

'When a child witnesses the kind of violence in dog-fighting staged by people,' said Cynthia Bathurst, director of the charity 'Safe Humane', 'they can become desensitised to pain and suffering, less able to empathize, and more willing to accept physical harm.'

Dog-fighting is undoubtedly disgusting and immoral. But with Chicago police statistics indicating that most dogfights take place in low-income, high-crime areas of Illinois, there are obviously broader social factors to consider before we instantly condemn all involved to a fiery Hell. Just as with the twinned miseries of narcotics and street gangs, dog-fighting is tied up in unresolved wider issues of class, community and education.

'Most of the kids we see at public school who have attended a dogfight live in minority areas,' reported Robyn Barbiers, also of the 'Anti-Cruelty Society'. 'It is amazing how some kids who live in certain zip codes have never heard of dog-fighting, while other kids know as much about dog-fighting as we do.'

We might never know for certain exactly how deeply involved Gerald was in this subculture. The line between truth and myth might always remain blurred. We can also never know whether dog-fighting was something he might have eventually grown out of naturally. He was, after all, still a young man of twenty-seven when dogs were still a part of his life. Chicago officials are aware of cases were such young men have outgrown such tasteless activities, with some even turning completely against it.

Derek Brown, a former leader of notorious Chicago street gang the 'Vice Lords', was once a chief promoter of dog-fighting in the city. Through a process of maturity and a short prison sentence, he became a reformed character.

Now in his thirties, he works as a youth mentor helping deter other kids away from his past life.

'Back then, I treated my dog like a piece of meat,' Derek admits. 'If my dog lost, I would leave him there to die and would go get another dog to fight. I know better now. When you know better, you do better.'

For her part, Lisa doesn't deny that Gerald was involved in dog-fighting. Understandably, she isn't exactly thrilled about addressing the subject either. I can sense her discomfort when I try to ask her about it. Previously, she has publically apologised on Gerald's behalf for anything unsavoury he may have gotten himself into. She also expresses a belief that many of the stories about him have been intentionally fabricated and sensationalised.

'There has been a lot of exaggeration,' she told me. 'Most of the stories came from both Stan and Donnie, and 95% of that shit was bull...I confronted Donnie about it on the phone one time and he denied it and said he was misquoted. But I told him he was a liar and not to call us ever again...They sold those lies for around $400. That's all it took.'

Considering the length and detail of Donnie's reported revelations to the press, that would be some misquote! I would hasten to point out here that I myself did attempt to track down Donnie Pendleton to allow him the opportunity of offering his side of the story. Unfortunately, a homeless person in Milwaukee is not the easiest figure to locate from an office in West Yorkshire, even with the best will in the world.

'And Stan Johnson tells so many lies,' Lisa continued, 'you never know what to believe from him.'

Gerald McClellan was never a saint. There is no definitive proof that he was once a monster either. So, what are we left with? A collection of violent stories that may or may not be true to any degree; a man now hated by thousands of people who have made up their minds of his guilt based purely on hearsay and their own emotions; a man incapable of defending himself against such accusations, and his sister who really shouldn't have to defend herself against any of it. That's just the way it is.

During the course of writing this book, Lisa told me that Gerald had been asking persistently for a puppy. With all of his beloved old dogs now long gone, he yearns for a new pet to hold and cherish and call his own. Lisa is considering letting him have one. For the sake of all involved, let's hope that those old horror stories don't hold much truth.

14

A Ho-Ho...

'Sweet is the voice of a sister in the season of sorrow.'
Benjamin Disraeli, ex- Prime Minister.

During the many phone calls I share with Lisa McClellan, Gerald is in the background. At times I am just aware of him. He will make small interjections and interruptions here and there as Lisa and I speak. I have gotten used to the tone and rhythm of his voice. He is audible if not always comprehensible.

On other occasions, he will be a noisy source of chaos that makes the phone call both difficult and interesting at the same time. He will bark demands at Lisa from somewhere nearby, his pitch rising and falling sharply, never sounding aggressive, but often sounding as though his request demands urgency. On these occasions, my heart bleeds for Lisa. I have come to envision her as the mother of a demanding 170lb man; a 170lb man who used to be her big brother. Even with all the love and patience of a saint, she must be exhausted.

'Lisa, Lisa, Lisa!' Gerald's calls drown out whatever Lisa was trying to say to me.

'Just a second, Wayne,' Lisa said again and she turned away from the phone. 'What, Gerald?'

Whatever request he made was indecipherable to me, but Lisa understood and she hurried to serve him. When she returned to the phone, I asked why he was so agitated.

'He wanted a soda and he said I wasn't moving fast enough,' Lisa explained.

'Did you just call me a bastard?' Gerald hollered from behind her, sounding genuinely insulted.

'No, I did not call you a bastard, Gerald,' Lisa pulled away from the receiver again.

'Why did you call me a bastard?' Gerald snapped, sounding every bit like an offended infant.

'Gerald, I said "fast enough", not bastard.' Lisa pleaded. 'Sorry about this, Wayne.'

I assured her that it was fine, I offered to call back at a more settled time. My pen was scribbling notes on my pad, my ears wide open, my eyes moist for what I was hearing. For me, the emotion is beyond explanation – is he him? Is he really him?

'I can't believe you called me a bastard!' Gerald squawked, or something like it.

'Gerald,' Lisa appeased again, her calm demeanour somehow never breaking for a second. 'I have told you, I did not call you a bastard. Now, you must treat me how you want me to treat you. Do you understand?'

Gerald muttered something and seemed to relent.

Lisa and I continued our conversation in relative peace for several minutes. Soon though, Gerald became agitated again. He wasn't saying anything in particular that I could decipher. He was just a bouncing ball of distracting energy in the background.

'Hang on, Wayne,' Lisa excused herself again. 'Let me just get him something to occupy him.' Lisa left me on the line for several seconds whilst she found something with which to distract the former world champion prize-fighter. She tossed him something. 'Here, Gerald, have a ho-ho.'

'What's that?' Gerald sounded puzzled.

'A ho-ho,' Lisa said.

'A what?'

'A ho-ho.'

'A what?'

'A ho-ho.'

'A what?'

'A ho-ho. A cake bar.'

'A cake bar,' Gerald must have gathered up his treat. He was hushed now; placated.

'There's another one in your lap,' Lisa told him – a double distraction. Then into the phone, 'Go on, Wayne; what we're you saying?'

At times when Gerald was in this mood, I felt completely in awe; not of the champion I had grown up fascinated by, but by the sister who has devoted her life to his wellbeing. Long after such calls ended, I would lay in my bed in Yorkshire and wonder what was going on in that house on Wyandotte Street in Freeport, Illinois; that house that Gerald proudly paid cash for when he signed his first deal with Kronk. When he made that purchase, he must have felt like a king. He must have felt certain it was just the first of many properties he would acquire and that each one would be bigger and fancier than the last.

How does Lisa accept such responsibility, such permanent pressure, without ever complaining? Far from complaining, she even shrugs off compliments. When I am moved to tell her how incredible she is, she dismisses it. Truly, she just sees everything she does every single day as her sisterly duty. She doesn't need or expect praise for any of it.

'When we were younger, Gerald and I fought like cats and dogs,' she told me, and I could believe it. 'Gerald was always a very selfish person with a big ego. He was like that before he got hurt, and that definitely hasn't changed. But he always had a good heart and he would have given anyone the shirt off his back if they needed it.'

Facetiously, I asked how Gerald did with the ladies back in the day. A good looking, confident, professional boxer – he surely can't have struggled for female attention.

'Oh, Hell no!' Lisa laughed. 'That boy screwed every single one of my friends; every last one.'

That made me laugh. With my own thick streak of male bravado, I felt strangely proud of the G-Man for getting his while he could. I wondered out loud whether enforced abstinence bothered him now; after all, the man was only twenty-seven years old when he was rendered unfit for action. I asked Lisa, cautiously, if her brother is ever allowed to see women these days.

'Not sexually,' Lisa said outright, catching my drift. 'I mean, he has women come to visit him sometimes, like friends. Even some of his ex-girlfriends visit him from time to time. But not like that.'

Suddenly, loudly, playfully, Gerald called out in the background, 'I'm a virgin!'

I broke out laughing. Lisa laughed too. Gerald laughed with us. For that split second, it was like Gerald was just a man again, just one of the guys playing around. It was heartbreaking.

As we moved on from topic to topic, I asked how involved Gerald's other sisters, Sandra and Stacey, are these days. After all, Gerald seems to be permanently in Lisa's protective care. At forty-eight years old, she is still plenty young enough to desire and deserve a social life, a romantic life, a life outside that of 'caregiver.'

'Stacey backed off within the first two years of Gerald getting hurt,' Lisa explained. 'She is still there if I really need help, but I try not to ask.'

I asked how much time Sandra spends with the champ these days.

'None,' Lisa answered. 'Not any more she don't. How can I make someone do what they don't want to do? Besides, if you make someone do something that's not in their heart to do, they'd resent him and not care for him properly. So, I just do it myself.'

This is a harsh but pragmatic way of looking at her situation. I have learned that Lisa is a realist – with her, things are often black and white, no gray areas. The world is not ideal and she won't pretend that it is.

Lisa was married between 1997 and 2003, but the relationship ended in divorce. I asked whether she felt the constant responsibility of being her brother's custodian had played any part in the breakdown of that marriage.

'Not from mine and his point of view,' Lisa said. 'But my husband's mother did sometimes get involved and say that I didn't have time to take care of my husband 'cos I was too busy taking care of Gerald...I do still get along very well with my ex-husband and with his new wife. They visit us from Denver sometimes and they are like family to me always...We take our grandchildren on holidays together, me, him and his wife. I love her too.'

I found this endearing. I have never come across divorcees who have retained such a healthy, amicable relationship. I know my own parents would still degenerate towards killing each other if they were left to share a room for five minutes. Such animosity is useless and toxic. Lisa's way is clearly better for all involved.

Lisa does have another longstanding male companion. Ironically, the other man in her life is also called Wayne. We both laughed at that coincidence and I laughed more when she admitted that she drives this other Wayne crazy with her moods – 'I can honestly believe that,' I joked.

'But Gerald really loves Wayne a lot and Wayne gives Gerald a shave and a haircut every week,' Lisa added. Then she joked, 'He just won't go away.'

The couple have been together for over twelve years and knew each other from childhood. Even after all that time, Lisa tells me she won't let Wayne live with her fulltime as she doesn't believe in co-inhabiting outside of marriage. It felt good to me, knowing that she and Gerald have another constant, positive figure in their lives. Still, it didn't seem right that so much of the responsibility of Gerald's care falls on Lisa.

'If he was still champ, everyone would still be around him,' I said, venting my own sense of injustice.

'You better believe it, they would,' Lisa replied. 'I'm so used to being on this journey by myself Wayne, that it don't even bother me no more. It used to, but don't no more. I look at it like this: I remain solo, I don't ever have to worry about being disappointed. My body hurts and I'm beat. I drink my coffee and keep going.'

My heart thumped for her again. Imagine this being your life from age twenty-six. Gerald was definitely not the only one who lost that night.

'Never change, Lisa,' I told her. 'As difficult as you can be at times, you're brilliant.' I said that and I meant it.

Lisa doesn't sleep much. I know this because our conversations often take place at strange hours, even accounting for the time difference between us. Often, she takes to her kitchen in the small hours and begins cooking up great pans of food – collard greens, steak and potatoes, cornbread and pork chops – enough to feed a small army. Considering that she and Gerald are the only permanent residents at the house, and even if Gerald has retained a hearty appetite, I wondered if cooking was therapeutic to her.

'Sometimes I guess it is,' she said. 'I do my thing at night while it's quiet.' I took 'her thing' to mean cooking and cleaning.

Conversations like this moved me no end. Lisa at her most open and amiable is quite a thing to be privileged to. She told me about her four beloved grandchildren and I could feel the love and pride radiating from her - family is everything. I felt happy for her then. But at the same time, I wondered where it would all end for her. As Gerald ages, surely his needs will only grow, his mental state will deteriorate, his endless demands on her time will only extend. And Lisa will age too, eventually. Surely, even with her heart as big as Illinois, even with her incredible resolve and her unshakeable faith in a divine goodness guiding her through each day, surely even she must tire at some point.

'Do people ever advise you to consider putting Gerald into care?' I asked cautiously.

'Some people have said that,' she said, 'especially my own doctor because of my own health issues.' (Lisa was diagnosed with a heart problem in 2007). 'But it will NEVER happen,' she added quickly, 'this is part of my everyday life, so what can I do about it?'

I took this as a rhetorical question and didn't offer an answer. I just sat there thinking about Gerald eating his ho-ho cake-bar like a placated child, and about Lisa cooking up late night hotplates when she really should be resting, and I thought of all the savage attacks that the holier-than-thou boxing fans launch so frequently against the McClellans on so many platforms for Gerald's alleged but never proven sins. I just felt sad and sorry. But pity is something I know that Lisa would never stand for.

I thought about how I had set out to write 'The Gerald McClellan Story' and how more and more it was evolving into the *Lisa McClellan Story*. As unintentional as that crossover had been, I was beginning to understand now that it had also been inevitable. In her own way, Lisa herself is a piece of boxing history. Inside, I just hoped with all my heart that my little book could do something to help them. I hoped I could make a difference.

15

The Arabian Prince

'A man paints with his brain and not with his hands.'
Michelangelo, Artist.

An accumulation of hard punches in an exceptionally violent fight; the accidental clash of heads in round nine that caused Gerald to reel away and momentarily sink to his knees in pain; or, a sinister underworld plot of poison instigated by a powerful love rival. The suggested reasons behind McClellan's terrible injury range between the probable, the possible, and the profoundly sensational. As I continued my research for this book, I spoke to a man who offered another explanation.

Tarick Salmaci was another Kronk fighter and Emanuel Steward protégé. Known as the 'Arabian Prince', he was a number one ranked amateur in the late 1980's and a top professional contender in the 1990's. He was also Gerald's club-mate and regular sparring partner. He would later star alongside Rocky himself, Sylvester Stallone, in the highly popular television series, *The Contender*. Mr Salmaci is now president of a successful real estate company in Michigan – it's nice to know that not all ex-fighters land on life's scrapheap.

Speaking to me from the States, Tarick explained his relationship with the G-Man, the Kronk, Don King, and shared his belief that there was a longstanding, underlying factor affecting Gerald's health.

'I first met Gerald when I was 16yrs old at the Kronk gym in Detroit in 1988,' Tarick said. 'It was during the time he turned professional and signed with Emanuel Steward. I was still boxing as an amateur at Kronk. I didn't start sparring with Gerald until 1991-92. I was top rated amateur at the time and Gerald was world champion. So sparring with him really helped me become a better all around fighter. Gerald was a middleweight and I was a welterweight. Emanuel would still have me spar him despite the weight difference.'

'My style of boxing is a boxer/puncher and I had a lot of foot movement. This would throw Gerald off a little bit in sparring. As you know, Wayne, styles make fights. For some reason, my style would give him problems. I think it was the foot movement. Emanuel would always mention that to me. Although, I know Gerald could've easily knocked my block off had he really tried. He once caught me with that left hook to the body. I didn't fall, but I folded and had to take a minute break to get my breath back. Nevertheless, sparring Gerald was a huge benefit for me because when I would get into the ring with amateurs my size, I would easily walk through them. I thank Gerald for that.'

'Gerald had an off/on relationship with Emanuel. In the beginning, things seemed all good. As time went on, it seemed Emanuel and Gerald didn't see eye to eye. This is the reason I believe Gerald left Emanuel after signing with Don King.'

'This incident happened two years before the Benn fight. Gerald and I were sparring at the Kronk gym and I hit him with a solid jab in between the eyes. The punch was nothing major, but solid. Gerald put a hold to our sparring session claiming that I had thumbed him in the eye. As he was telling me this, he was blinking really fast and non-stop like he did during the Benn fight. I noticed it at the time, but never thought anything of it.'

'After our sparring session, we were in the locker room and Gerald walked up to me and said, "Tarick...you didn't thumb me...I'm man enough to admit it, but you didn't thumb me... You hurt me and I'm man enough to admit it"... I thought to myself, how could I have hurt him with a jab wearing 16 oz gloves? It was odd.'

'Fast forward a couple years later, and I happen to be at Don King's office in Florida negotiating a promotional contract to sign with Don King, and at the same time Gerald was there training for the Benn fight. Gerald had just recently signed with Don King and Emanuel Steward was no longer Gerald's trainer. So Gerald was in Florida training for the Benn fight with another trainer.'

'One day while at Don King Productions offices, I ran into Gerald in Dana Jamison's office. Dana was or still is the vice president of Don King Productions. I walked into Dana's office when I seen Gerald there. I walked to say hello and we started talking about his upcoming Benn fight. This is probably 2 weeks before the Benn fight. I asked Gerald how much he was making for this fight and he told me $100,000. I replied that the amount was ridiculous and that Benn had a huge name in England and the fight was taking place there. I told him that he should be getting way more than that for this fight. Gerald replied, "That's what I'm saying"...'

'As soon as he said that, Dana Jamison (Don King's Vice President of Boxing Operations) walked into the office. She overheard part of our conversation. She got upset with me and began telling me that I have no right telling her fighters how much they should or shouldn't be making, etc... I just ignored her and walked out.'

'Gerald and I hung out a few times during his camp before he left to England. I watched his fight on TV while still in Florida. When I seen Gerald start blinking the way he did during and after the Benn fight, I said to myself, that is exactly the way Gerald was blinking a couple of years ago when he put a hold to our sparring session claiming that I thumbed him. Again, Gerald later admitted to me in the locker room that I didn't thumb him and that I had hurt him. The topic of the blinking never came up between Gerald and I because I never thought anything of it until after Benn fight.'

'I don't agree [that the clash of heads caused the blood clot]. It may have triggered it, but I don't believe the clash of heads caused it. I believe it was just a matter of time before a blow to his head would trigger the blood clot and whatever else was wrong in his brain.'

16

The G-Man Junior

'It should have been stopped when he was knocked out'a the fucking ring.' Gerald's son on the Benn fight, to me, October 2017.

Gerald McClellan Junior did not only take his father's name. He also inherited his brooding good looks and his fiery personality. With tattoos covering every inch of his toned torso and creeping up to his face, the junior G-Man would not look out of place in a music video for rapper 50 Cent. Young Gerald was not the easiest person to pin down for interview, but on the few occasions we did exchange messages, I found him to be a very polite and approachable young man. Nevertheless, his thoughts on what happened to his father definitely lean more closely towards the conspiracy theories of his aunt than to the undetected medical condition explanation offered by Mr Salmaci.

'It should have been stopped when he got knocked out'a the fucking ring,' Gerald Junior, who also goes by the nickname 'King Black', asserted. 'And the ref was clearly in on the shit.'

I couldn't help wondering how much of young Gerald's opinion had been influenced by his aunt. He was, after all, only six years old when his dad came home a different man. I also couldn't help wondering how much his own life had been affected by what happened.

'I just got out the feds,' he told me, referring to his recent stay in prison. 'I been in the ring since I was sixteen. Been in and out, but trust me I got pure champion blood...I'm about to get back to it.'

Gerald Junior had followed his father into a professional boxing career. Interestingly, he had at one point been coached by Gerald's former corner-man, Donnie Pendleton. Gerald Junior is also certain that had his father been fit and well enough to be guiding his career, then he too would have reached world champion status by now.

'I've seen every one of my father's fights,' Gerald Junior went on, 'that's kinda what my style is like.'

Much like his Aunt Lisa, young Gerald doesn't seem the type to convey a shred of self-pity. This is a family of individuals who just assess each situation, say it how they see it and get on with things as best they can. Still, I couldn't help feeling sorry for him. His father is still around and young Gerald does visit him with his own children. But no one can ever know what might have been if circumstances were different.

I have seen pictures of the two McClellan men posing playfully together during the son's visits to Lisa's home. There is one picture in particular that caught my eye; one where Gerald Junior is tensing his bicep whilst Gerald Senior tests the muscle's quality with his fingers. He cannot see, but he can feel. It is a moving image and one that drew my mind instantly to another photograph I had seen recently – a picture of another father and son posing proudly together; the father in that picture was once a boxing champion too; the son in that picture has followed in his dad's footsteps too; but there the similarities end. Nigel Benn and Conor Benn have lived very different lives to those of the two Geralds.

17

The Darkness of the Destroyer

'I'm happy because, you know what, I came out the other end.' Nigel Benn.

Glory is fleeting.

Darkness had fallen. On the broad stretch of land that is Streatham Common, there is nothing to break up the emptiness. A black Bentley sat idle with its engine running. Inside it, alone, sat a Godless man, a man at the end of his rope. He was tired of all this; tired of that self-loathing ache that gnawed away at his inners, tired of being a slave to his own impulses, tired of the addictions that drove him to keep on making the same mistakes. He was tired of hurting the ones he loved the most and he was tired of knowing that he would keep on doing it. As a fighter, he had never met his limit for physical pain. As a man, his threshold for the emotional kind had now been breached.

He swallowed a handful of sleeping pills, washed it down with a gulp of wine. From the exhaust pipe at the car's rear, he had trailed a length of hose. The radio was on low. The car filled steadily with sad music and toxic gas. The fighter closed his eyes and waited to drift off to pastures new. He waited to be counted out.

Nigel Benn had staged five more fights after beating Gerald McClellan into a coma. It has often been written that the 'Dark Destroyer' lost his killer instinct after that fight. Evidence of this is sparse – he knocked out both of his next two opponents in 1995. He also continued calling out the exceptional Roy Jones, though a lucrative showdown never materialised. Three consecutive defeats in 1996 brought his career to a disappointing end. But even so, I would disagree with the popular idea that he was a completely spent force. His succumbing to old rival Sugar Boy Malinga, where he lost his title, was a lacklustre struggle which could have gone either way. His next two defeats both came against Irish warrior Steve Collins, who had by then emerged as probably the most dangerous super-middleweight on the planet. Even then, one of those defeats came as the result of a badly twisted ankle – these were hardly soft losses indicative of a faded fighter on the slide. By the time he hung up his gloves, Nigel Benn would probably still have been capable of holding his own against most of the division's top ten.

Nevertheless, Benn decided he had had enough anyway, and who could blame him? With a hard-earned fortune in the bank, no lasting injuries from his decade of ring wars and a loving family waiting at home, he was in a dark place. The playboy lifestyle of party-drugs and extra-marital sex was not making him happy. Cheap women selling their cheap stories of cheap lust to cheap tabloids probably weren't making his wife very content either.

'I never felt he was a complete bastard,' Caroline said in the late 90's. 'Just partly one...For years, I felt as though he would leave me at the drop of a hat, but I stuck with him because I felt he needed me. I was his closest friend...Nigel was an emotional wreck...He was living from fight to fight.'

And now there were no more fights for Nigel. He was a fighter without a fight, a warrior without a war. So here was, the once but never again king had reached the end of the road, his once irrepressible spirit no longer willing to go one more round. But as he sat alone in that vehicle, enveloped by self-inflicted despair and car exhaust fumes, something happened - the hose fell out of the exhaust. This did not happen just once, but three times. Each time Nigel slotted that hose into the pipe and climbed back in his car to die, that hose somehow freed itself and fell uselessly away.

Was this a sign of divine intervention, or more a sign that Nigel wasn't very proficient at sticking a hose into an exhaust pipe? Nigel took it as the former rather than the latter. Coming to his senses, he gave up on giving up and drove home to his mansion. Soon, he would be hearing the voice of God calling him to salvation. Soon, he would be born again as a child of Christian faith.

'I just wanted someone to put their arm around me and say, "you're gonna be alright,"' Benn said of the attempt. 'I had low self-esteem, so if women showed me attention I hung onto it...I had a sex addiction. People say "is sex really an addiction?" But I know it's an addiction, because I didn't care if they were size ten or size twenty-two.'

At least he's honest.

'Maybe if I had Caroline from the beginning, I could have cleaned up everything in boxing,' Nigel said in praise of the woman who stuck by him. Perhaps Caroline is Nigel's version of Lisa.

'She made me get rid of all the hangers-on who were bleeding me dry...I cheated on Caroline. I was still really messed up in the head. I didn't trust anybody...The only time I ever felt at ease was when I was boxing. I was crying. I wanted to commit suicide. I had a nervous breakdown.'

In the early days of his retirement, Benn had swapped boxing for a career as a DJ. Obviously, this entailed spending frequent late night hours surrounded by drink, drugs and females – the devil and all his works. Having survived his suicide attempt, he and his faithful second wife packed up and moved to Majorca, Spain. The intention was to put some distance between him and the old temptations. It was on Caroline's bidding that they began attending church.

'All my addictions from drink, from sex and smoking weed all went like that,' Benn clicks his fingers to describe the immediate impact of reciting the Prayer of Salvation. 'I was set free from everything.'

Before long, Benn had so embraced the spirit of the church that he swapped the pew for the pulpit and began preaching the good word himself. When the picturesque setting of Majorca no longer satisfied him, he and his wife moved further afield, to sun-soaked Sydney, Australia. Admirably, Benn began working with underprivileged youth and operating as a form of counsellor through the church he belongs to.

'My new addiction is serving people,' he gushed, 'whether it's through boxing, or in my role as a volunteer assisting people with their marriages or helping those less fortunate.'

Contentment permeates through Benn's words now. There was, however, one less fortunate soul he was yet to extend Christian aid to. As Benn spent the first decade of his retirement finding God in sunny places, Gerald McClellan sat waiting for God in a wheelchair in Freeport, where the weather is a little more temperamental. It is no surprise that bad blood continued to linger between the McClellan family and the newly ordained punching preacher.

'One of the last things I remember reading about the fight in one of the tabloids was, "We want Benn dead, we want his money". You know what? I've grown up since then,' Benn commented several years after the epic battle.

There is no doubt that much of the lasting tension was drummed up by the media as an attempt to score cheap headlines here and there. It is also perfectly understandable that Lisa held a deep resentment for Nigel, and particularly for the remark he had made on leaving the hospital that morning in 1995.

'Rather him than me,' Nigel had shrugged dismissively. He had actually said that, even with Gerald laying just a few rooms away, in clear and present danger of losing his life.

'I wished he was dead,' Lisa admits. 'That's honestly how I felt. How can a man who almost took someone's life sleep at night?'

Years passed, one after another - one anniversary after another of that fight trundled by. Every so often, the boxing magazines would run an article about how brutal and tragic it was. Occasionally, there would be an update of Gerald's condition, complete with photographs of the handsome young fighter juxtaposed against images of how he looks now – a disabled dependent. Every so often, there would be a fundraiser in his honour; a well meaning few would try to scrape together enough cash to make a dent in Gerald's ever mounting medical debts. Sometimes, a well known fighter such as Roy Jones or Muhammad Ali would make a donation. On one occasion, Joe Frazier, Evander Holyfield and Bernard Hopkins all flew out to Freeport to visit the G-Man. But, more than a decade after their war to end all wars, Nigel Benn and Gerald McClellan remained strangers to each other.

Suddenly, in 2007, it was announced that an event was happening. Suddenly, twelve years after the battle, there would be something like a reunion.

18

Something Like a Reunion

'He's no Christian.' Lisa McClellan on Nigel Benn, to me, Nov 2017.

If 'The Gerald McClellan Story' had been a work of fiction for a Hollywood script, then the reunion between our lead protagonist and his former rival would have been integral to the plot. It would have been a scene of raw emotion in the final act, no doubt providing closure for our characters and for us, the audience. But this is real life. Human drama does not obey script conventions. The Benn-McClellan reunion of 2007 was anything but cinematic.

I have watched the video footage of that reunion many times. It was, after all, the subject of a popular television documentary. The footage of the moment that Benn and McClellan were brought back together is very often shared on internet boxing forums and I am always interested in reading the comments which quickly and inevitably pile up underneath. Without fail, the video provokes emotional exclamations from fight fans across the cyber-world.

'Now, this is what you call respect!'

'So moving! These are real men.'

'This is beautiful.'

I watch with keen interest as well-meaning comments like the above ping in beneath the video. I have always resisted my own urge to comment on such posts of this particular episode. All things are subjective, I know. But from the very first time I ever watched that reunion footage, I did not see it the way these other gushing observers did. Long before I first began talking to Lisa, long before she discussed her perspective on all this with me, I couldn't help feeling that something about this 'reunion' just seemed a bit off. I found it awkward and uncomfortable and difficult to watch. But that was just my humble opinion. Interestingly, when I finally reached the point of asking Lisa how she really feels about Nigel Benn and that reunion, I found my opinion vindicated.

I watched and re-watched the footage several times whilst writing this chapter. Gerald slouched in his wheelchair, dressed smart-casual with a baseball cap on his head, reminds me somewhat of a large child in a pushchair.

'Lisa, we in London?' he asks his sister as they come into camera shot. I wonder how many times he had already asked her that question that very day.

'Yes,' Lisa answers her brother, her patience never faltering. They progress towards the end of the long aisle where Nigel Benn is waiting. For Lisa, it must have felt something like a ring walk.

Nigel crouches beside the wheelchair and takes Gerald's hand in his. His expression appears to show sincere discomfort at what he is seeing - perhaps the bleak reality of it all is just now dawning on him. Camera's click rapidly and audibly in the background. Gerald, for reasons known only to himself, wants to know Nigel's full name. Nigel and Lisa spend the next couple of minutes repeating it in turn into Gerald's ears.

'Nigel Gregory Benn...Nigel Gregory Benn...Nigel Gregory Benn...'

Gerald spends the remainder of the conversation speaking to Nigel through Lisa. In a way, it is almost as though Nigel isn't even there. With his head tilted towards his sister, Gerald asks whether Nigel looks 'mean or sad.'

He asks Lisa whether she thinks Nigel is sorry it happened. He asks, curiously, which religion Nigel follows. Then, his voice suddenly pitching, Gerald squawks painfully, 'Lisa, this man almost took my life!'

For both Lisa and Nigel, that was about enough. Nigel stood up and walked slowly away with tears in his eyes. Still in camera shot, he began weeping loudly with a sudden release of tension. Lisa simultaneously instructed the cameras to stop rolling. She knew better than anyone that her brother was getting agitated. His feelings were more important than any film reel.

'They weren't happy,' Lisa said, 'but I told them that was enough.'

No matter how many times I replay this footage, the same questions swim in my mind. Why did that reunion take more than twelve years to happen? Why did it take place in front of a television crew, rather than in a more private and dignified setting? Granted, it was part of a fundraising event which Gerald and his family would benefit from financially. Still, it seemed somewhat crude and ingenuous to me; the way that Lisa and her aunt had to wheel Gerald in his chair down that long corridor, with cameras flashing and tracking their every step, to meet the waiting Nigel Benn, who stood suited and booted in front of yet more cameras. Could there not have been a completely private meeting first? Should the cameras and filmmakers not have been given their pound of flesh after Lisa had been given chance to first lay eyes on the man who had effectively changed her life? It just seemed wrong to me. I wanted to know how Lisa really felt about it.

'You ask me what I think about Nigel Benn now,' Lisa said to me, 'well, the answer is, I *don't* think about him. The truth is, he has done nothing for Gerald. That whole reunion wasn't even arranged by him. It was all arranged by Kevin Lueshing (Benn's agent). Kevin did all that.'

I asked if there was anything Benn might be able to do now to improve her opinion of him at all. Lisa, as always, did not hold back.

'I don't want anything from him now,' Lisa replied, that familiar fire scorching her tone again. 'It wouldn't be from the heart anyway, so I don't want it. If he did something now, it would just be so he could say to the world, "Hey, look at what I'm doing for Gerald." It wouldn't be from the heart. Like when we were in England, he was all teary and apologetic. Then soon after we got back to Freeport, he was back to giving interviews talking about how he barely even thinks about it now, and back to bringing up stuff about Gerald and the dogs. So, it was all fake.'

I mentioned to Lisa that Nigel now lives in Australia and is a Born-Again Christian. Lisa gave a little incredulous scoff.

'He's no Christian,' she said.

It is hard not to sympathise with Lisa's point of view. After all, Benn has made disparaging remarks about Gerald on many occasions since their first encounter. He even dedicated a small portion of his 'An Audience with Nigel Benn' stage tour to sharing stories of Gerald allegedly shooting dogs and living a 'gangster' lifestyle. As recently as 2015, Benn made comments in a televised interview for *Ringside Magazine* in which he again dismissed the whole saga as something that rarely crosses his mind now.

'I rarely think about it to be honest,' Benn shrugged. 'And it's only discussed when someone brings it up. It's part of my life that's behind me and I don't really dwell on it.'

These are hardly the sentiments of a disciple. It is a free country, however, and Benn is certainly not under any obligation to shower affection and regret upon Gerald just because their fight ended badly. On the other hand, more cynical observers are also well within their rights to question the Christian values of one who can come across as so insensitive. Just as it was with that old 'Rather him than me,' remark in '95, sometimes it is better to say nothing at all.

My A-Level in Psychology certainly doesn't qualify me to psychoanalyse a complex character like Nigel Benn. At times though, I have wondered whether his vilifying of Gerald is a sort of defence mechanism. Perhaps there is less pressure to feel guilty or remorseful if he tells himself that the man he hurt was a monster. Or maybe Nigel really doesn't think so deeply into things. In either respect, both men knew exactly what they were going up against that night, didn't they?

'I know that Nigel was on steroids when he fought Gerald,' Lisa added, almost out of nowhere. This took me by surprise. 'Kevin Lueshing told me himself while we were in London that Nigel was using steroids.'

I was already aware of rumours regarding Benn and performance enhancing substances. I knew that this allegation had been thrown at Benn in the years after the McClellan fight. Much had been made of Benn's sudden collapse on the way to the dressing room that night, despite him being a raging ball of energy just moments earlier in the ring. Some believed this was his ploy to avoid been drug tested immediately after the showdown. Stan Johnson had also made an unsubstantiated claim that blood recovered from one of Gerald's boots had tested positive for a banned substance. According to him, this was Benn's blood. As is usually the case with Stan, he couldn't back up what he was saying with hard evidence. Nigel, of course, denied any wrongdoing.

I thought long and hard about this information. If Benn's agent really did confide in Lisa that his man had been 'juiced up' at the time of the McClellan fight, it seemed unlikely that he was ever going to admit it publically after all these years, and least of all to 'little old me'. After giving it much consideration, and for my own reasons, I decided against contacting the Benn camp for comment. As with every other revelation in this book, I guess people will make up their own minds.

For his part, Benn did not try to take credit for organising the reunion event. He didn't give credit to anybody for it else either. In Benn's eyes, the reunion was all down to the man upstairs.

'Just one thing I want to say to you,' Nigel told the press on the eve of the fundraiser. 'This is nothing to do with me or Kevin. Nothing. It's to do with God. It's for the ultimate glory of God...If I had done it for any other reason, it would have been all about deadwood. And deadwood means all about *my* glory.'

Regardless of the motives behind the organising of that reunion in 2007, Lisa and Gerald did benefit from it. The black tie dinner event in London raised several thousands of dollars in donations. British promoter Frank Warren personally donated $25,000 and, perhaps surprisingly, Lisa's old foe Don King later matched this donation with his own.

'Frank Warren made that kind donation,' Lisa told me. 'And then he said he was going to call Don King and suggest that he do the same. Don King donated $25,000 because Frank Warren asked him to. That was the only reason.'

So that was that. Something like a reunion had taken place. The documentary makers had their precious footage. Nigel Benn had given something back, ostensibly at least. Lisa and Gerald had a nice cheque with which to make a small dent in their medical bills and everybody could go back to life as normal, whatever that might be.

19

It Never Rains

'God never gives you more than you can handle.' Christian adage.

On December 31st 1998, New Years Eve, another monumental tragedy had struck the McClellan family. Genola McClellan, the beloved mother of Gerald and Lisa, was killed in a house fire in Freeport. As if the family hadn't suffered enough. If there is a God looking down on us, then he certainly has a strange way of portioning out the misery.

'We were devastated,' Lisa told me, the pain clear in her voice. 'Gerald understood what had happened, but he couldn't go to the funeral. It was too much for him.'

Emotionally crushed by the loss of their mother, the mourning McClellan siblings were united in grief. However, the tragedy did nothing to ease the rift between the girls and their estranged father. In fact, it only led to more bitterness between the two camps. I asked carefully whether Emmit had been supportive through this dark time.

'Hell no!' was Lisa's answer. 'He never came to town. One thousand people were at my mom's funeral and he never showed up.'

I could see how Lisa would be hurt by her father's absence in such a colossal moment of need. I could also see why her father might not have felt welcome at his ex-wife's memorial service after all of the friction in the years prior. Most of all, I just wondered how Lisa made it through those turbulent years of the late 90's.

'It seems like Gerald got hurt and then everything just fell on you at once,' I said to her.

'Yes,' Lisa replied. 'And then our Nana died soon after our mom.'

God must be a real bastard, I thought. But I stopped short of saying it.

By hook or by crook, Lisa and Gerald made it through the 1990's. With their mother gone, their father estranged and Lisa increasingly becoming Gerald's primary caregiver, their circle was shrinking. Somehow, Lisa's resolve only grew.

'It's all in the way that my mom raised us to look after one another,' she said. 'And at the times where I feel like giving up and walking away, I feel my mother kind of tugging at me from the grave and letting me know that that's not what she would be pleased with.'

But the family's emotional roller-coaster certainly didn't end going into the new millennium. Just a few months after that 2007 reunion in London, Gerald and Lisa received another due invite. This time, their presence was wanted in California. Gerald had been inducted into the International Boxing Hall of Fame at the earliest stage of his eligibility. This is the most prestigious honour that can be bestowed on any fighter and effectively elevates him to legendary status in the eyes of fans and peers alike. For Lisa, the invite out to the West coast presented a dilemma. She wasn't certain that she could endure another long distance journey with Gerald, knowing how agitated and unsettled he had been during the recent trip to England – imagine several hours trapped in a plane with a confused and demanding man-child.

Lisa strongly considered leaving Gerald at home in Freeport with her sisters whilst she went to collect the award on his behalf. In the end though, her well-disguised sentimentality got the better of her and she decided it felt only right that Gerald attend in person. Once again, the inseparable pair would brave the journey together.

Despite Gerald suffering a violent seizure on the plane and Lisa been forced to complete the final leg of eight hours and six hundred miles from Phoenix in a hire car, the siblings finally made it to the award ceremony. With tears in her eyes, Lisa proudly accepted the accolade on her brother's behalf. Gerald, in his best suit and in his wheelchair, was present and correct under the watchful eye of his Aunt Linda.

'The G-Man was one of the bravest and most ferocious fighters I've ever seen,' said the commentator Steven Albert as he presented Lisa with the precious plaque. 'And it was a pleasure to call his fights.'

Seeing her brother receive deserved recognition from his beloved sport was a welcome, temporary boost for Lisa. But award shows and after parties are short-lived. They still had to face the long flight home to the realities of Freeport. Without a doubt, there would be more drama, more stress and more worry in the McClellan family's future.

2012 would be a particularly tough year for the McClellans. In the same year that Gerald's old mentor Emanuel Steward sadly passed away, the McClellan family was rocked by a series of problems closer to home. Terrifyingly, Gerald's health took a serious turn for the worse. Soon after his 44th birthday, he began complaining of severe stomach pains.

'He never complains,' Lisa said, 'Never. So I knew something must really be wrong.'

Something was wrong. After a trip to the Emergency Room, where the agitated Gerald had to be sedated, a test revealed that his colon was no longer functioning. This was a delayed by-product of his nervous system been impacted by his brain injury. The brain controls everything. All these years later, he was still suffering fresh pain from that fight.

After several tests and different opinions from specialists, the conclusion was a devastating one – Gerald's colon would have to be removed, forcing him to live the rest of his life with a colostomy bag. Surgeons had desperately looked for an alternative to removing the organ, with the possibility of an ileostomy been discussed. But further tests revealed that in the earliest days of Gerald's injury, a hospital feeding tube had spilled over into his abdominal cavity. As a result, parasites had attacked his inner lining, inflaming it and causing a painful bacterial infection known as peritonitis. The resulting surgery left enough scar tissue in both the large bowel and small bowel to make the desired alternate method impossible.

So that was that; Lisa would now have the added lifelong duty of monitoring her brother's bowel activities through a colostomy bag. She would also have to go through the immediate nightmare of explaining to Gerald why he now had a bag attached his abdomen.

'What I tell him today, he won't remember tomorrow,' Lisa said at the time. 'So tomorrow I'll have to tell him again. I've been trying to make it a normal part of our conversation every day for the last couple weeks. I've explained it to him and I said "well, what do you want me to do?" And he said just call the doctors so they can do it. So he understands. But remembering the day after when he wakes up and has that bag on, I don't know how he's gonna react.'

As if this latest setback wasn't enough to deal with, Lisa also had the simultaneous worry of her sister falling into poor health. Her elder sister Sandra had been struck down by kidney failure, with her organ operating at only 10% of its required function. Their brother Todd bravely stepped up to the plate to offer one of his kidneys. In the end though, it was Sandra's own daughter who became the donor after tests showed her to be a perfect match.

This meant that three members of the McClellan family were now in hospital at once, all three undergoing major surgery – Gerald was hospitalized in Chicago, whilst Sandra and her daughter were laid side by side in Wisconsin. For Lisa, the family's leader and linchpin, this meant several hours of travelling in opposite directions to visit her recovering loved ones. When the trio finally came home on the mend, it was Lisa who helped nurse them back to health.

'Sandra went into renal failure,' Lisa told me. 'Her daughter gave her a kidney. 'These were stressful times. I just kept going. What else can I do about it? I took care of all three of them…They are in very good health these days.'

In the aftermath, Gerald did come to accept the colostomy bag as just another sad part of his life. It is also just another unfortunate part of Lisa's. Both Sandra and her daughter are still around and Lisa remains in touch with both of them. For such blessings, I am sure she is thankful.

As I absorbed all of this information and tried to get my head around exactly how much this brave woman has been through, my mind spun back to something Lisa had said to me in one of our earliest conversations – 'God is going to provide for me always.'

There is strength in faith, as they say. It is probably a miracle that Lisa has retained hers.

20

Wipe Out

'The mind is like an iceberg; it floats with one-seventh of its bulk above water'. Sigmund Freud.

The world will never know exactly how Gerald McClellan's brain injury has affected his perception of the world. He cannot communicate coherently enough to explain how far his sense of reality has been distorted. We can see the damage from the outside looking in, and we can wince at it. We can never know for certain how it feels from the inside looking out. Even the most learned surgeons and scientists of our time can only theorize on the experience of navigating the world with a brain so badly damaged. The brain controls everything. There are some things that text books cannot teach us.

My best hope of gauging some understanding was to speak to someone who knows this experience firsthand. With that in mind, I got in touch with another young fighter whose career had been cut tragically short by injury. Like Gerald, this brave young warrior had suffered a subdural haematoma. Like Gerald, this man is still affected by that injury every day.

On 12th September 2014, British light-welterweight prospect Jerome 'Wipe Out' Wilson suffered a brutal knockout defeat in the sixth round of his bout with Serge Ambono. The devastating final blow caused a subdural haematoma, the same thick clotting of blood between the brain and skull that left Gerald in his present state. Mr Wilson, of Sheffield, spent ten days lost in a coma. A quarter of his skull had to be removed. Thankfully, he survived. Unlike Gerald, Jerome still has the ability to see. He can also communicate coherently. But there are multiple other lasting impacts of the injury. Jerome was kind enough to talk to me about the disorientation and despair of what he went through. I started by asking him what memory he has retained of the fight itself.

'I now only remember my brother Marvin picking me up in his car,' Jerome began. 'And on arrival at the arena we were greeted by my dad as we walked in. My brother was carrying my sports bag. I remember chatting to a few fans and friends and then made my way into the changing rooms. I got changed, found the music man to pass my music on to him. On the way back to the dressing room I was stopped by my partner, her dad and my three year old daughter, who had never been to a boxing event before. I had a short chat with them and then took my daughter Serenity around the changing room and introduced her to some of the fighters and my team, just to try and make her feel a bit more relaxed before turning her back over to her mother.'

'After sorting out all the usual things before a fight, I was changed and focused on the task at hand. I next remember talking and bantering with my coach while hitting the pads (and occasionally his stomach and head, jokingly). I have no more memory of what actually happened in real life. But I have memories of a different reality in which I lived and experienced. That replaces what really happened next, until I awoke from my coma ten days later and tried to piece together what really happened versus what I thought happened. It was a very profound, surreal and unsettling experience.'

Jerome's account of his comatose state is the stuff of nightmares. He imagined conversations with family members and hospital staff that never took place. He convinced himself that he had been hurt as a result of fall out with one of his friends. He believed that the doctors and nurses were holding drunken parties on the hospital ward at night and saw the image of one nurse with her face made up like a clown. He believed the medical staff had let him fall out of bed and sleep on the floor. I felt immense pity for his suffering and great respect for his bravery. I also couldn't help wondering whether Gerald might also have experienced such terrifyingly realistic 'living dreams.' For all we know, he might still experience them.

Jerome eventually had a plate fitted in his head to fill the gap of several inches left in his skull. But even over three years after the injury, he still suffers severe ongoing symptoms. His moods fluctuate erratically, he grows tired suddenly and his self-confidence has been badly dented. Like Gerald, he has also suffered stomach and chest problems as an offshoot of the brain damage. He is struck by bouts of chronic acid reflux, abdominal pain and breathing issues. The brain controls everything.

I asked Jerome his thoughts on the medical professionals who so frequently call for boxing to be banned outright.

'I have a love-hate relationship with many aspects of boxing,' Jerome answered honestly. 'Boxing I love. The business side, I hate with a passion. More transparency and support is needed. And people with a conflict of interests shouldn't be allowed to influence or control too much of a fighter's career, to give a fighter the best chance of doing better in the sport.'

I knew that Jerome was here referring to his own subsequent struggle with the boxing authorities to receive due financial assistance. But my mind went immediately back to the self-serving methods of Don King. Just like Gerald, Jerome could no longer earn a living to provide for his family. Just like Gerald, he was left out in the cold.

'You don't get much needed support from boxing authorities,' Jerome continued. 'And this needs looking into in a big way to see how they can help fighters appropriately and adequately as soon as possible and for as long as possible. Many of the injuries affect the rest of a fighter's life, not just for an allotted time period. It isn't just about throwing money at the problem. It's about being there to support them, offer guidance and show them they are valued as people. That is not done right now. You are made to feel like an enemy and a burden, having to fight for what you deserve. Support should be offered naturally without any friction or discomfort attached to it...I've had no insurance pay out, but we're dealing with that legally, so hopefully may get to the bottom of that in a few years. It's a long process...The board have given me a bit of money in the past, but should do a lot better than they have.'

'The sport won't ever be banned,' Jerome went on. 'To think it would be is laughable really! I do understand why medical professionals call for it to be banned because of the devastating, life changing effects I live with on a daily basis. Yes, tragedies happen, as they do in other sports. But many positive things can be attributed to boxing.'

I asked Jerome whether he feels any animosity towards the opponent who inflicted the damage upon him.

'I have no animosity towards him about the fight itself,' Jerome replied graciously. 'I know this kind of thing can happen. I'd like to think he won fair and square. But the immoral and disturbing acts afterwards just make me feel belittled and sad really.'

Jerome was referring to his opponent's questionable actions in the ring immediately after the fateful knockout. Ambono celebrated in the ring and made a tasteless, taunting gesture to the crowd, making a sweeping motion across his throat with his gloved fist, even as paramedics were scrambling to revive Jerome. I couldn't help thinking of Nigel Benn bounding euphorically around that ring in London as Gerald lay strapped with an oxygen mask.

'The disrespect he showed me as I lay dying on the ring canvas, and to my family, is really unforgivable,' Jerome carried on passionately. 'It still grates on me from time to time...The brain is a strange and powerful thing. I'm a shadow of who I used to be. But I'm able to add to mine and my family's lives in my own way. I'm blessed, man.'

I asked Jerome a variation of a question I would later pose to Lisa McClellan: If he could somehow go back to night of that fight, knowing everything he knows now, would he stop himself getting into that ring?

'If I knew the life changing and devastating outcome, yes, it would definitely prevent me from getting in the ring that night to fight,' Jerome said. 'I wouldn't want to intentionally put my friends, family and supporters under so much stress and fear, not knowing if I would survive, or even if I did survive, what physical and cognitive condition I would be in. Your loved ones hold that fear inside them every time they see you enter that ring to engage in battle.'

I couldn't thank Jerome enough for giving me his time and speaking so openly to me. I also found myself wondering how Gerald would have responded to that final question.

There is no way I could ever ask Gerald himself now – his injury has had a much more formidable impact upon his ability to communicate than in Jerome's case. In time, I decided I would do the next best thing. I would ask Lisa what she believes Gerald would have said.

21

Running

'I run on the road long before I dance under the lights.'
Muhammad Ali, Legend

Picture a kid running. He is skinny and undeveloped, bandage-wraps tied sloppily on his tiny hands. At first, he is running just for the heck of it; because his dad told him to, because his older brother is doing it, because he likes the idea of being seen as a fighter. His little ego devours it. At school, the boys fear him and the girls are fascinated by him. Nobody gets in his way. He keeps on running up that hill.

He keeps on running until his muscles elongate and harden and hair grows on his top lip. It is more than a hobby now; a passion, a calling. The wraps on his hands are fastened tight and clean now. He runs on and shoots hooks and crosses at the air. He runs until girlfriends and old friends fall away by the roadside. He runs until plastic trophies and cheap neck medals sit on his parents' mantelpiece; Tommy Hearns posters are pinned to his bedroom wall. He keeps on running. His chin is tucked in close to his chest, his tight eyes focused ahead on future glories. Nobody gets in his way. He keeps on running.

He keeps on running until he runs all the way clear of Freeport; that small town can't match his stride now. He loves it, but he strides beyond it, running. He runs until he comes through the doors of the Kronk Gym in Detroit. He runs until he is in the arms of Emanuel Steward. Now, he is running under the wing of a Hall of Famer, a trainer of champions. Nobody gets in their way. He keeps on running.

He runs through contenders. He runs through champions. Chin down, eyes up, hooks and crosses like atomic bombs only he controls. Nobody gets in his way. He runs until Emanuel loves him like a son and moves him into his home. He runs until a belt of gold and glory glints from his waist. He runs until they know his name in countries he has never run through. Lights are flashing; his music blasts, love and war come quick and easy. He might never stop running.

He keeps on running until Emanuel can't keep up and falls away by the roadside. No stopping. Nobody gets in his way. He keeps on running and nobody can keep up. He keeps on running and he knows he is unstoppable. He keeps on running clear of everyone and everything. He keeps on running clear, towards London...

As I worked on this project, my friendship with Lisa had at times been a tempestuous one. We were somehow prone to silly misunderstandings and short, heated quarrels over virtually nothing. Often, it was just the six hour time difference between the US and the UK, along with our separate busy schedules, that frustrated us both. Other times, arguments just seemed to pop up unexpectedly. There was a brief squabble when she accused me of talking over her. There was another brief falling out when I took the liberty of speaking to her nephew, Gerald Jr, without asking her permission first. Lisa saw that as me going behind her back. I explained that I was simply conducting necessary research and, as she still hadn't signed my publisher's contract, I really had no binding duty to run anything by her at all. Standing my ground only seemed to anger her more.

'You better check yourself, Wayne,' she would say. 'Sometimes I think you're a good guy. But when you piss me off, I feel like saying "fuck you and fuck your book."'

I checked myself. I was always quick to apologise.

'If I'm already stressed and on the edge of my seat with Gerald,' Lisa explained, 'and then you come rushing me, I just don't have time for it.'

After each of these spats and misunderstandings, there would be a stalemate. Lisa would ignore my calls and messages for a few days and I would feel stressed and anxious. It was agonising for me, knowing that she really was a primary and precious source of information required to make this book as true and honest as possible. At times I felt drained and frustrated by her proclivity for taking me the wrong way. It was all the more difficult to figure out given that Lisa can very often be a most likable, talkative and pleasant character.

'I can't figure out your personality,' I told her once. 'On the one hand, you're a funny, caring, religious person; on the other, you come across as hard and short-tempered.'

'I'm always hard,' she replied matter-of-factly. 'Always been the same.'

Bits of the blame for most of our minor wrangles probably rest on both sides – I can undoubtedly be a first class prick, as many ex-girlfriends would gladly testify. But Lisa also has a fiery temper and some serious trust issues. I reiterate that this is understandable given what she has been through. But the more we talked, the more her old line of 'I trust no one, dear,' became a sort of catchphrase. On another occasion when I brought up her lack of trust, Lisa replied with panache, 'I trust no one, and it's not an issue.'

I liked that one. It sounded cool. I also had to appreciate that this woman was effectively opening up great portions of her life story to me, some English guy she had never met. Of course, it was going to take time for her to build faith in me and my intentions. I had to be patient.

Regardless of such obstacles, we were both obviously passionate about telling the McClellan story. I was certain we had a melting-pot for creating something truly special with this project. This is boxing history, after all. But from such a broth there would inevitably fly occasional spits and sparks. It would be a far from simple recipe to master. We would endeavour. We would learn to deal with each other's personalities.

From the off, I said this is a story which transcends boxing. It is a chronicle of loss, family strife and human suffering. I am familiar with all of these. Forgive me if I appear to digress here momentarily from the story at hand, but I feel that the following few paragraphs will give the reader some insight into my occasionally turbulent relationship with Lisa McClellan over the course of producing this book.

My closest loved ones would tell you that I am far from the calmest of characters (what writer is?). I hope to think I am a genuinely nice person. I am definitely more passionate than most when it comes to the things I truly care about, sometimes to my own detriment. All in all, I am a well-meaning guy, if I do say so myself.

But spectacular folly is also a personal speciality of mine, and if alcohol is involved, then so much more dramatic the fall. I try my best not to drink these days, but drink is always there when a sad and angry man needs it the least. It is the most accessible means of shutting down and hiding from reality for a period of time. You twist the cap, you tilt the bottle and you fade away...It's gorgeous.

One weekend whilst working on the book, I lapsed into a three day bender which was never going to end well, if it ended at all. It happened to be Halloween weekend and I was in a devilish mood. Without going into details, this brief, explosive venture into self-destruction involved two trashed hotel rooms, a fallout with a hotel manager, a scuffle with a taxi driver and enough vodka to fell an elephant. I had lost my way again and I would suffer for it later.

In the midst of this bedlam binge, I missed several calls and a stream of frustrated messages from Lisa. We had things to discuss and she couldn't understand why she couldn't reach me all of a sudden. By the time I came to my senses, she had reached a junction of anger and despondency. She accused me of being ignorant and a fraud and just another name in a long list of people who had let her down. She had emphasised her anger by blocking me from her social media pages. She also informed me, quite dramatically, that she no longer considered me a friend: 'If we're friends, then why can't you answer a call...Hello...What happened to you...The least you could do is reply...I'm about to get pissed off...Hello?'

With my liver taking a standing eight count and toxins leaking from my pores, I fell hard and fast into the worst hangover Mankind has ever known. I drown in an unforgiving sea of anxiety, self-loathing and despair. It would be days before I could look anyone in the eye again. Hell was the few inches inside my skull where only I can wander. Drink is the devil and all his works.

'I have a very stressful life,' another message from Illinois read. 'I don't need this.'

The alcoholic mist all too slowly began to rise. My mind began to clear. I needed to find my feet again, put one foot in front of the other. Obviously, re-establishing contact with Lisa was a priority. There was so much I wanted to say to her. I wanted to explain that the trigger for my going AWOL had been the fact that I was missing my daughter, Casey.

I miss my little girl painfully every day. She is the great love and obsession of my life, as every child should be to every parent. But when seasonal celebrations like Halloween come around, the pain takes on a raw intensity. I get to watch uselessly as other parents dress their children in cute costumes, carve pumpkins and go out 'trick-or-treating.' These banal little activities are priceless in terms of bonding and forming cherished memories. They are crucial and adorable and precious.

Meanwhile, I get to sit alone, wondering if my baby is having a good time, knowing that another man who is NOT her Daddy is getting to bask in her pretty smile, that smile *I* created. The pain is unbearable. And all of this because her mother doesn't like me very much. I know there are countless men in my situation around this ever crumbling nation and I feel truly sorry for every one of them. But who cares? Certainly not the government or the 'family' courts.

Every man deals with such an onslaught of emotional pain in his own way. Me? I have a tendency to lock myself away in a hotel room, annihilate myself with booze, junk food and self-pity, and wait for the whole terrible, beautiful ordeal to blow over. Birthdays, Christmas, Easter, Fathers' Day – these are all personal agonies where men like me become detached from the world around us. As the tempest rages inside us, we can but tie ourselves to the mast and pray not to sink so deep that we never re-emerge. It is crazy how brutally your own love can savage you.

And so it was, 'Happy Halloween, Wayne,' - I checked into a hotel, I ordered bad food and tipped back bottle after bottle until the pain and outrage faded to a docile snigger. Days passed...

This time I drank myself senseless. I drank so much for so long that I could barely stand. I lay confused and inebriated, tangled in hotel bed-sheets, a white towel covered in vomit beside me. I curled into a foetal position and listened to a young Asian couple arguing in a neighbouring room. My head thumped, mind racing, pulse twitching. Every nerve in my body rattled, wishing they would stop; please, let it all stop.

Ironically, it was my own sister, Kay, who eventually came searching for me. She was worried that no one had heard from me for a few days and she knows me well enough to read the signs of a meltdown in Wayne's World. Just as Lisa can sense when her brother is festering towards agitation, just as she can tell when one of his terrifying seizures is imminent, so my sister can sense when the black cloud has fallen around me. Feeling weak and lost in that God-awful no man's land between sobriety and paralytic, I took a taxi back to Kay's place and slept on the floor. My heart would still be broken when I awoke, but at least it would no longer be Halloween. The streets wouldn't be filled with happy families dressed as ghosts. I wouldn't have to feel like such a lonely fucking loser again until Bonfire Night.

I could have tried to explain all this to Lisa McClellan at the time. I could have told her that I have family-shaped problems too, that I really do understand at least some of her anguish; that this is what families do to each other; they take your life and they break your heart – love is pain.

I could have tried to tell her all this, but I didn't. It wasn't her problem, after all. She was helping me write a book, she was not my counsellor. Instead, I simply sent her a couple of short emails to break the ice. The first one was ignored outright. The second earned a curt reply. There followed a brief and slightly awkward phone call between us where I did all the talking. More messages and calls followed and Lisa softened with each one. Gradually, we returned to whatever strange little relationship we had previously struggled towards. She unblocked me from wherever I had been temporarily blocked and we moved on. We were moving forwards again, not running by any means, but limping maybe. I vowed to myself that I would learn to deal with the pain differently. I had turned a corner and nothing would get in my way.

Eventually, Lisa and I *would* end up having a real heart to heart about the situation with my daughter – in fact, we had several conversations about my situation and how it affects me. Lisa being Lisa, she even insisted on contacting my child's mother on my behalf. There was something surreal about having the sister of one of my boyhood idols speak so candidly to me about my deepest personal pain. None of what she said seemed be of token or platitude value. Lisa would revisit the subject often and gently encourage me to talk about it. When I did open up, I felt the terrible pressure in my chest significantly lighten, if only for a little while. The many words of support she gave me will never be forgotten.

By the time I reached the end of this project and I was ready to submit my manuscript for publication, I realised I would truly miss speaking so often to my friend, Miss Lisa McClellan.

22

A Flicker of Hope

'I once was blind, but now I see.' John 9:25

On Boxing Day 2017, the day after Christmas Day, Lisa McClellan called me. She wanted to tell me about something exciting that had happened. Naturally, I couldn't wait to hear it.

'Gerald will see again,' she told me. 'His blindness is in his brain, not in his eyes.'

Lisa has always kept the faith that her brother will one day enjoy having vision again. Now, almost twenty-three years after his world went dark, there was suddenly a flicker of hope. Lisa told me that she has recently been in contact with a progressive stateside doctor who specialises in nurturing the brain through diet.

'This new doctor has been advising me, Wayne,' she explained. 'He told me to remove all of the gluten and nitrates from Gerald's diet and feed him more of certain vitamins to help detox him. He believes this can strengthen the brain.'

Lisa has been taking the good doctor's advice, and she has already noticed dramatic results. Firstly, Gerald has been remarkably much more alert and responsive than usual. But then, on Christmas Day of all days, something potentially miraculous had happened.

'I got up yesterday,' Lisa began, 'and Gerald was sitting up in his chair. I kissed him on the forehead and wished him a happy Christmas and gave him his present to open. Suddenly, Gerald said to me, "Lisa, I'm scared." I asked him why he felt scared and he said, "Because I can see something flickering, like this..." and he made a sign with his fingers in front of his face to say that something was flashing. He said, "Lisa, I can see lots of small green lights flickering in front of my eyes." The thing is, Wayne, as he said it, Gerald was sitting in front of the Christmas tree which I had decorated with all green lights. You know he always loved the colour green. So he was seeing the lights! Some of the light was getting through.'

This was incredible. Even a glimmer of good news was refreshing. After so many months of delving into so much sad and explosive material, I felt genuinely uplifted by this possibility of life improving progress for the McClellans. I also felt blessed that it had happened so close to me finalising my manuscript.

I hope with all my heart that Gerald's condition continues to improve. God willing, he will one day lay eyes on his sister again.

My one regret from putting together this publication is that Lisa and I were thus far unable to locate the mysterious Ms Maria Russey, Gerald's old flame from the 1990's. Given that more than two decades have passed since Ms Russey was involved with Gerald and Don King, taking into account that King allegedly warned her off ever contacting the McClellan family again, and assuming that Maria' last name may well have changed at least once in the event of marriage, it is probably no great surprise that she proved difficult to find. We cannot even be certain that Ms Russey still resides in the United States.

On the off-chance that Maria should stumble upon this publication, I would like to take this opportunity to encourage her to make contact, either with myself or with Miss Lisa McClellan. I am sure that Gerald would still be delighted to hear from you after all this time.

'He would love it,' Lisa adds.

23

The Hardest Game

'The boxer is doing what's expected of him; bleeding from the nose.' Harry Carpenter, Boxing Writer and Broadcaster

Glory is fleeting.

In boxing, more so than in any other major sport, the biggest and brightest stars often fall crashing and burning spectacularly from the pinnacle. Even as we feel pity for the fallen, there is something tragically fascinating in every story; every fable of the man whose destiny drags him from rags to riches and back to rags again. We watch with wide eyes. We cannot help but look, pry and investigate his dramatic demise whilst lamenting on just how great he might have been, if only and if only and if only...We are only human, after all. As the old adage goes, 'Whom the Gods wish to destroy, they first call promising.'

Through sheer talent and unimaginable dedication, these exceptional men fight their way out of humble beginnings. Be they from a Brooklyn ghetto, a Filipino slum or a Manchester backstreet, no boxer reaches the top of his trade without enduring immense physical, mental and emotional pressure. It is such a cruel twist of fate that the rewards of their courage are so often short-lived.

Muhammad Ali, the self-proclaimed 'Greatest', defiantly boxed his way out of poverty and government-endorsed persecution to captivate the entire world throughout his glittering prime. If a more passionate and naturally gifted man ever walked this Earth, I'm yet to read of him. Still, by the time Ali retired, a long and painful slide into serious illness was the bulk of what awaited him. It stings to imagine that irrepressible spirit trapped inside a degenerating shell. The king of kings deserved better than that.

Ali's successor to the throne was Mike Tyson. Precocious king of the ring through the mid to late 1980's, he wound up spending much of his fighting prime languishing in prison. Bad decisions and a reckless lifestyle also saw him squander much of his early potential, along with a financial fortune beyond the comprehension of us mere mortals. These gloomy examples are far from being exceptions. The hardest game is littered with such sad stories of fallen warriors. But are any more tragic than the tale of Gerald McClellan?

From bankruptcy to crime, depression and death, cataclysmic personal loss seems to haunt the icons of our beloved sport. There remain an almost infinite number of less high-profile cases across the vast history of boxing: Leon Spinks went from a champagne lifestyle to living in squalor, as did Iran Barkley. Randolph Turpin was the toast of England when he upset the legendary Sugar Ray Robinson, yet he finished his career working hard labour on construction sites and died by suicide at age thirty-seven. Sugar Ray himself, frequently cited as the best boxer ever, was reportedly broke by the time he retired. Alzheimer's and diabetes would be his next opponents. Rocky Marciano, the Great White Hope, died in a plane crash the night before his forty-sixth birthday. The brave Vinny Paz gave the performance of his career and then broke his neck in a car accident. Arturo 'Thunder' Gatti made his millions the hard way and was then found dead in a Brazilian hotel room at age thirty-seven. Long serving heavyweight Trevor Berbick swapped gloves for cuffs when he was jailed for raping his children's nanny. He would later be brutally murdered by a member of his own family. Yemeni-Yorkshireman 'Prince' Naseem Hamed reigned supreme as boxing royalty in the 1990's, but he would eventually slip off his throne and land in a prison cell when his dangerous driving left another man seriously disabled. Ex-middleweight champion Michael Nunn is currently serving a fifteen year prison sentence for narcotics supply. Ali's old rival Sonny Liston fell in with the Las Vegas mob and died of an apparent heroin overdose. British heavyweight hero Frank Bruno was briefly sectioned under the Mental Health Act. Canadian George Chuvalo suffered the torment of outliving three of his five children, losing one to suicide and two to drugs. Riddick 'Big Daddy' Bowe served prison time for spousal kidnapping. Tommy 'The Duke' Morrison landed a starring role in the fifth Rocky movie and then died tragically young of AIDs. The great Joe Louis retired owing millions to the IRS and spent time in a psychiatric hospital. British 'boy next door' Ricky Hatton had a brief stint in rehab and spoke openly of contemplating suicide. Promoter Frank Warren survived been shot in the back on a London street. Even Nigel Benn, as we have read, would at one point almost succumb to his inner-demons by attempting to take his own life.

The list of hard luck stories from the hardest game goes on and on. And what do past glories count for then, once they are but mere film-reel and photographs and there is really nothing left?

Some might argue that the many personal disasters listed above are simply down to fate and that tragedy is far from exclusive to boxing. There is certainly a degree of truth in that. Others would suggest there is a lack of guidance in place to cushion a fighter's transition once his punches no longer pay the bills.

This point was emphasised by another ex-fighter, my friend and former club-mate, Gary 'Five Star' Sykes. Gary began boxing amateur at age fourteen and won a string of national titles before turning professional. He spent ten years as a star of the domestic scene, twice winning the British super-featherweight title and beating the likes of world champion 'Million Dollar' Crolla before retiring at age thirty-one. Sykes spoke of a crisis of identity after hanging up his gloves.

'When all you've been for over seventeen years is a boxer, then that's gone, and there's no coach or manager, there's no fight to get ready for, then you have to work out who you are. It's just you and the rest of your life.'

The harsh and fickle nature of the fight business is summed up just as philosophically by other fighters too, especially those at the fading end of the limelight. Mike Tyson again offers a prime example. As a man who must have snapped every branch of the tree on his own chaotic fall from grace, Tyson once looked at his formerly treasured championship belts with disdain and scoffed, 'I can honestly say, I bled for garbage.'

Popular heavyweight Gerry Cooney made the same point, albeit somewhat more eloquently, when he said, 'All of the sports have a safety net, but boxing has none. So when the fighter is through, he is through. While he was fighting, his management was very excited for him. But now that he is done, that management team is moving on.'

Chicago sportswriter Bob Verdy also hit the nail on the head when he wrote, 'The bell that tolls for all in boxing belongs to a cash register.'

The message from each of the above is the same one that echoes through the annals of time: after the bell, once the party is over, once the champagne and the quick money has stopped flowing, once all of the good-time girls have gotten dressed and gone home, once the imitation gold on the title belt turns to rust, the fighting man is left alone in the universe. If he is lucky, he might have managed to cling to someone special enough and sincere enough to stay by his side in the aftermath. For Gerald McClellan, that special and sincere one is his sister, Lisa.

But is that enough? What about *her* life and how it was irreparably affected? Has boxing done enough to support Lisa as Gerald's 24/7 caregiver?

The first time I ever spoke to Lisa McClellan on the phone, with Gerald vocal at her side, emotions almost drown me. Lisa McClellan is a good person who has been dealt a terrible hand in life. It goes without saying that I hold massive respect for the limitless devotion she has shown for her brother. I am thankful that she was open to conversation with me from the moment I introduced myself and laid out the intentions of my project. It even struck me that she seemed glad to have someone showing an interest in her brother's story again, that over two decades later, he wasn't been completely forgotten.

I think back to that first phone conversation often. At first, I was just happy that she could understand my strong northern England accent (Americans have a tendency to think that all Brits speak like Londoners). When I became a bit star-struck at realising the G-Man was actually present beside her, I think she was amused. It soon became a three-way conversation and I felt honoured to be speaking with the two of them – Gerald seemed obsessed with knowing my height, my weight, my middle name and why I gave up boxing. Just like that, they became real people, flesh and blood, rather than images on a television screen or in a newspaper. When Lisa first put me on the phone to Gerald himself, I could hardly sit still. I can never thank her enough for that and I will never forget it.

But from the off, I could also sense a fiery side to Lisa's personality (perhaps a family trait). I would obviously get much more familiar with this side of her as our project progressed. There is strength in Lisa's voice, but also frustration, pain, perhaps even anger. She lives life with her guards up and who can blame her?

As our conversations became more regular, both online and by phone, I quickly came to like and respect her. Quickly, I went from referring to her as 'Ms McClellan' to 'Lisa' to 'G-Girl.' I gave her that nickname playfully and I think she liked it.

On another occasion, I tried put Lisa at ease by insisting she could trust me. I wanted to convey that financial gain was not my motivation for this book, passion was. I will never write about any subject that doesn't set my heart on fire – life is too short for that, and there are enough sell-out writers in the world to fill a boxing ring. I told her that the *Gerald McClellan Trust* would make more money from this book than I would, and I meant it. Lisa's simple reply was, 'I trust no one, dear.' Coming from someone who has dealt with the likes of Don King, I couldn't possibly take that with offence.

'We struggle,' Lisa went on. 'Nobody knows how it really is here but us. We have been burned enough.'

Maybe I'm too sensitive, but that hit me like a straight right to the chest. Lisa is not a professional fighter. She never chose to risk her life or her lifestyle in a boxing ring. She never laced up the gloves and prepared for war with anybody. But in the space of around twenty-eight minutes one London night, her life was changed forever. Inside ten violent rounds, her beloved older brother was transformed from world conquering athlete to severely disabled dependent. The fight purse and the insurance money quickly evaporated under the glare of relentless medical bills. Boxing and its 'yes-men' and its hangers-on promptly left the party, and Lisa was left to pick up the pieces.

Gerald knew the risks and they were his to take, not hers. Lisa's devotion knows no bounds; he is her brother, after all. But what is Gerald McClellan now to the rest of the world? An occasional nostalgic newspaper headline, a sporting statistic, a story to reminisce over with friends at the bar ('you remember that fight, man...')? Is he just another tough kid whose luck ran out? Or, is he just another victim of the hardest game?

A few short weeks before the Benn fight, Gerald's aunt, Loretta Pruitt, awoke in the night with a terrible feeling; a premonition, a sense. She wasn't quite certain of the details, but she knew for sure that she needed to contact Gerald. Whatever it was, it involved him.

Her nephew, the champ, was in Florida busy getting ready for his next big fight. Soon, he would be travelling to England to fight some British guy who was supposed to be tough. Loretta called Gerald and told him not to go – she felt something terrible was going to happen if he went.

'Our aunt is not a psychic,' Lisa told me. 'But she is a very religious woman, and she really felt that something was wrong.'

Supernatural gift or a wise woman's intuition, Aunt Loretta's concerns didn't penetrate Gerald's guard. Certain that his destiny was in his own hands, he dismissed it. Soon, he would be boarding a plane for London. Soon, the morbid prophecy would be fulfilled.

After Lisa had relayed this anecdote to me (another unexpected but fascinating tangent from one of our many phone conversations) I felt compelled to ask another question.

'If you could somehow go back to that night in February 1995,' I said carefully, 'and you could go into Gerald's dressing room before the fight, knowing everything you know now, would you stop Gerald getting into that ring?'

The answer seemed obvious. But with Lisa McClellan, you just never know.

There was a long pause on the line. Perhaps Lisa was looking at Gerald beside her, observing her beloved and blind fifty year old brother, the man who has not laid eyes on anything since the night in question over twenty-two years ago. Maybe she was looking at the faint scalpel scar on his skull that runs all the way down to the surface of his brain tissue. She might have glanced at the colostomy bag on his side, or closed her eyes and listened to the sound of his irrational babbling. Perhaps all of the painful days and sleepless nights of twenty-two years were spinning in her mind, along with all the debts and all the stress and all of the bitter feuds. Maybe she was picturing herself now, somehow coming magically through the doors of that London Arena dressing room in 1995; coming through those doors and finding her big brother, gloved up and ready to go to work, a young-again warrior adorned in green and gold, his eyes all seeing, a confident young man so certain that this was just another night, another fight, another prelude to glory.

Would she stop him climbing into that ring? Would she tell him what the future held for both of them if he did?

Finally, Lisa answered.

'He wouldn't let me stop him,' she said it as though she had just tried, as though she had just returned to her present self from a mental voyage to 1995. There was another brief pause.

'He wouldn't let me stop him,' she said again. 'He would want to get in that ring. He would want to fight.'

Bibliography of secondary sources and referenced texts:

Benn, Nigel, *The Dark Destroyer, The Autobiography of Nigel Benn*, Blake Publishing, London, 2017

Mitchell, Kevin, *Observer Sport Monthly, The Guardian, Fighting For Life Article*, Sunday 4th November 2001

Newfield, Jack, *Don King Unauthorized Documentary*, PBS/Frontline, 1991

Berkow, Ira, *New York Times, A Boxer's Darkness Article*, November 12th 1995

Clarke, Gabriel and McKenna, John, *The Fight of Their Lives Documentary*, ITV Broadcasting, UK, 2011

Razak, Bobby, *Fallen Soldier Documentary*, IMDb, Side Control Media, UK, 2013

BBC Broadcasting, *Television News Archives*, Various, UK, 1995-1996

ITV Broadcasting, *Television News Archives*, Various, UK, 1995-1996

Smith, B, *Gerald McClellan Article*, The Detroit News, 1996

Hoffer, Richard, *Dark Days a Year After Nearly Been Killed in the Ring Article*, Sports Illustrated, March 4th, 1996

Halling, Nick, *Bradley Stone Article*, The Independent Newspaper, Wednesday 27th April 1994

London Real TV, UK, Nigel Benn interview, 2016

An Audience with Nigel Benn Tour, 2012

Thomas Gerbasi, Boxing Scene Article, 2012

The Free Library, Nigel Benn, Caroline Benn article, 1999

Mitchell, Kevin, Atonement for Benn and McClellan Article, The Guardian, 4th February 2007

O'Shea, Bernard, The Price of War Article, The Independent, 2012

Hutson, Wendell, Englewood, Auburn Gresham and Chatham, Crime and Mayhem, Urban Animals, 2012

Coming soon from Warcry Press

'John L Gardner – The Forgotten Champion'
with Nick Towle

He was the Hackney Rock, the 'Mini Marciano', king of the British and European heavyweights, yet somewhere down the line John L Gardner became the forgotten champ. Terrorised by a brutal father, shunned by his peers, his was a torrid childhood in the deprived East End where his only friends were his doting mother and an Alsatian called Victor.

The boy from Hackney rose from obscurity to become the man they all feared, but fate always seemed to get in the way.

At his peak, Gardner was nigh-on unbeatable. He faced down the gruesome Paul Sykes, went toe-to-toe with Ali.

He fought the law, battled a rampant gambling habit and ultimately stared down his most resilient foe - the 'Big C'.

He came at opponents like a swarm of bees, finished careers, reduced strong men to whimpering wrecks. Referees had to step in to end the abuse.

A pressure fighter to his very core, Gardner squeezed the pips out of men who came with big reputations that were left in shreds.

He was the ultimate professional on the cusp of world domination, but was ultimately let down by the very men meant to safeguard a precious talent. He paid the price and then fought for his life - in the very truest sense ...

ISBN: 978-0-9955312-9-1

Coming soon from Warcry Press

'Tales in Pugilism'
by Jamie Boyle

A unique look into the lives of some of the key players in
and around the boxing world. Featuring many well known
faces, we'll be asking how they first got involved in boxing?
and what it means to them. With many inside
stories it reveals a side to boxing one often doesn't see.
Written by Jamie Boyle author of Paul Sykes books,
Unfinished Agony and Further Agony, it will be a hard
hitting boxing book for sure.

ISBN: 978-1-912543-03-8